WELCOME
TO THE REST OF
YOUR LIFE

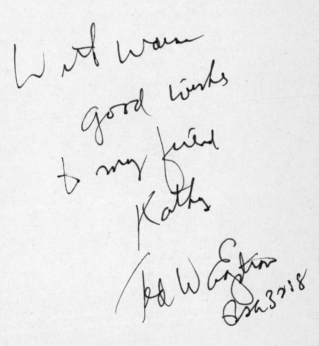

With warm
good wishes
to my friend
Kathy

Ted W Engstrom
Isa 3718

WELCOME
TO THE REST OF
YOUR LIFE

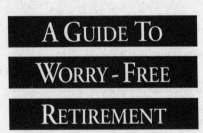

A GUIDE TO

WORRY - FREE

RETIREMENT

TED ENGSTROM
and Norman B. Rohrer

ZondervanPublishingHouse

Grand Rapids, Michigan

A Division of HarperCollinsPublishers

Requests for information should be addressed to:
Zondervan Publishing House
5300 Patterson Avenue Southeast
Grand Rapids, MI 49530

Library of Congress Cataloging-in-Publication Data

Engstrom, Theodore Wilhelm, 1906–
    Welcome to the rest of your life : a guide to worry-free retirement /
Ted Engstrom and Norman B. Roher.
      p. cm.
    ISBN 1-310-40531-9
    1. Aged—Conduct of life. 2. Aged—Religious life. I. Roher,
Norman B. II. Title.
BJ1691.E54 1992
248.8é5—dc
    2091-44667
    CIP

Printed in the United States of America

94 95 96 97 98 / DH / 10 9 8 7 6 5 4 3 2 1

To Dorothy,
who has shared
all of my four careers
—*Ted*

AUTHORS' NOTE

The guidelines, suggestions, and exhortations of this book are not meant to replace the professional advice of specialists in the field of finances, law, real estate, and medicine. If you have a medical or legal problem, by all means seek professional advice.

The message of this book is designed to show you that most doubts and worries about retirement can be resolved. Your attitude can determine many of the results. Remember, it is not what happens to you that spoils life but how you react to what happens. In everything, give thanks. Never succumb to the view that there is no way out and no answer available.

_____ CONTENTS

THE THIRD WAVE

People spend a third of their lives learning, a third of their lives working and a third of their lives . . .

How you spend that last third, commonly called *retirement*, is largely up to you. Five thousand people in America turned sixty-five today; tomorrow another 5,000 will join them. That's 325,000 candles on birthday anniversary cakes, a bunch of gold watches from their employers, choruses of "Auld Lang Syne" sung haltingly by fellow workers and then the sad trips home from the office to fill out the forms to apply for Medicare and settle into a rocking chair.

What's missing here? That's the subject of this book. Read on and discover secrets for making the last third of your life the most rewarding and the most spiritually fulfilling of all.

Grow old along with me!
The best is yet to be,
The last of life, for which the first was made.
Our times are in his hand.

Who saith, "A whole I planned,
Youth shows but half; trust God: see all,
nor be afraid!"

(Robert Browning)

FOREWORD

Retirement, it has frequently been said, is a concept not found in the Bible. The Scriptures rather give us examples of those who led full lives until the very end—like the warrior Caleb who at the age of eighty was still saying, "Give me this mountain" (Joshua 14:12).

Retirement from a paid career or profession is, however, a fact of modern life. World population is aging. Early in the next century one in every six persons will be over sixty-five years of age. Many who are coming to the end of their working careers are asking: After retirement, what?

At a grand opening for one of his restaurants, a reporter asked cowboy movie star Roy Rogers, "Roy, are you enjoying retirement?" Roy rather ruefully replied, "Not really." An old cowboy who was nearby spoke up. "I agree. Retirement is the tiresomest thing there is. 'Cause when you're doing nothing, you can't stop and rest!"

But retirement can be a time of continued fulfillment and growth. And this is the possibility that Ted Engstrom brings before us.

No one I could think of is better suited to write this particular book. Dr. Ted has already had many careers—as publisher, leader, manager, writer, and speaker. Thousands have learned from him about managing and mentoring and the use of time.

Since Ted's own retirement from the active leadership of World Vision, he and Dorothy have embarked on a new adventure. Ted finds time to play a good round of golf and to relax with friends. He enjoys being free from the constraints of executive leadership. He and Dorothy and their family are enjoying more leisure time to know each other deeply.

Yet Ted's life is still full of opportunities to speak and write and counsel. His wisdom as a board member is still much in demand. At the same time, he is helping younger leaders to set their priorities and put their organizational houses in order.

In this book, Ted Engstrom helps all of us who are near or into retirement to be good stewards of all that God and life have taught us. Someone has said, if you are wondering whether you still have a mission in life, try asking yourself, "Am I still alive?"

I commend this book strongly. It will help many to see that while we are alive we always have a mission.

LEIGHTON FORD
Charlotte, North Carolina

_____ **INTRODUCTION**

*I*n 1900 there were three million people in the United States over the age of sixty-five. Today there are approximately 30 million. By 2030 that figure will be 46 million. Senior citizens will then control one third of the vote in national elections. We are in better health than seniors have ever been, and we enjoy a surprisingly wide range of activities requiring both mental and physical exertion.

I reached my three-score-years-and-ten half a decade ago. Retirement has been the happiest time of my life. I want you to be able to say that, too, after you put into practice the suggestions of this book. Although there might be snow on the roof, there can still be fire in the hearth.

For too long, modern American culture has been preoccupied with the pursuit of youth. Senior citizens are not always held in the highest regard. Many struggle with low self-esteem, yet the Bible has a radically different perspective on youth and old age. It's the gray-headed person who is esteemed the highest. Senior citizens have a unique opportunity to make their greatest contribution during their sunset years.

Young people have misconceptions about anybody over thirty. A rock group refuses to allow anyone with gray hair into their concerts; a cool dude in Brooklyn said with great authority that to be old is to look through glasses smeared with dirt, to go around with cotton in your ears, boots on your feet, and gloves on your hands when you try to do anything constructive.

Contrary to the sometimes short-sighted perspective of younger types, much of the western world has been abundantly enriched by people with seniority. The graying of America is a tremendous resource for implementing God's plan to bless every person with the offer of salvation. As rest homes and nursing facilities expand to admit record numbers of the elderly, some of whom see longer lifespans as a curse of boredom and uselessness. But a worldview that focuses on God's unchangeable purpose sees the growing population of elderly believers as a significant resource expressly allowed by God for such a time as this.

How shortsighted is the following lament by two authors writing about people's advanced years:

> Crabbed age and youth cannot live together
> Youth is full of pleasance, age is full of care;
> Youth like summer morn, age like winter weather;
> Youth like summer brave, age like winter bare.
> Youth is full of sport, age's breath is short;
> Youth is nimble, age is lame;
> Youth is hot and bold, age is weak and cold;
> Youth is wild, and age is tame.
> Age, I do abhor thee; youth, I do adore thee.[1]

Have we got news for those writers! Our years might be yellow in leaf but the sap in the tree is still strong, the air crisp and alluring, and hope exciting and new every morning.

The Bible praises old age and promises honor for those who respect it. Leviticus 19:32 directs, "You shall rise up before the hoary head, and honor the face of an old man . . . ." (RSV) The Lord promises that the righteous shall "flourish like the palm tree, and grow like a cedar in Lebanon" and will "bring forth fruit in old age . . . (Psalm 14, RSV). And Proverbs 20:29 states that "the beauty of old men is their gray hair" (RSV).

Retirement might take us out of a familiar workplace, but think of all the new possibilities for spending our time. William James lamented that most human beings live far within their limits. "We possess powers of various sorts that we habitually fail to use," he said. "It is evident that our organism has stored-up reserves of energy that are ordinarily not called upon—deeper and deeper strata of explosible material, ready for use by anyone who probes so deep." He's right. The best books are yet to be written, the best paintings are yet to be painted, the best buildings yet to be built . . . .

Many of the following items were invented by people in their retirement: television, penicillin, polio shots, antibiotics, and frisbees. We were born before frozen foods, nylon, Dacron, and Xerox, and before radar, fluorescent lights, credit cards, and ballpoint pens.

We who are senior citizens were here before drip-dry clothes, before ice makers and dishwashers, clothes dryers, freezers, and electric blankets, before Hawaii and Alaska became states.

We were before plastics, hair dryers, the forty-hour work week, and the minimum wage. We got married first and then lived together in the biblical way.

Pizza, Cheerios, frozen orange juice, instant coffee, and McDonald's were unheard of when we were born. We were before FM radio, tape recorders, electric typewriters, word processors, Muzak, and electronic music.

In our youth, gasoline cost ten cents a gallon. If anyone asked us to explain CIA, MS, NATO, UFO, NFL, JFK, BMW, or ERA, we would have answered, "Alphabet soup."

And now here we are talking about the final third of life. We don't all enter it in the same way. Retirement can mean a traditional, full retirement or a phased retirement that takes a person out of the work force gradually. It can also mean cyclical retirement that takes a person from one job to another, even to a completely new career. Some people retire once, others retire several times, and still others never retire at all.

How do you plan to retire? Is volunteer work in your program? Is your goal to have more time for family, friends, or a hobby? Is it working part-time? Starting your own business? Or all of the above? Retirement is unique for each person. Only you can add the ingredients that will make it successful. Only you have the unique combination of experiences, personality, hopes, and expectations to make the retirement years all you wanted them to be.

The assuring words of Psalm 103:5 promise that a believer is "renewed like the eagle." The eagle, some naturalists believe, lives to be a couple of hundred years old. At one hundred, we are told, all of its feathers are changed, renewed. This is a wonderful picture which the Holy Spirit has given us of our renewal as we walk with the Lord.

We seniors are not always eagles, however. Philosopher Francis Bacon once noted sadly that aged people tend to "object too much, consult too long, adventure too little, and seldom drive business home to the full period" because they "content themselves with a mediocrity of success."[2]

Do Bacon's words describe you? If so, be prepared for some changes in your life as you read on. The future is as bright as the promises of God. Psalm 103 promises that the Lord forgives our iniquities and heals our diseases. He redeems our lives from destruction and crowns us with lovingkindness and tender mercies. He satisfies our mouths with good things, so that our youth is renewed like the eagle's.

I can hardly wait for the sun to come up. My days are full of special projects, board meetings, travel, sessions with clients for my management audit services, time with my wife, Dorothy, and our children and grandchildren, and a round of golf two or three times a month. If you've been dreading retirement, or if you are caught in lean and troublesome senior years, take courage. New opportunities lie ahead that you have only dreamed of before.

TED W. ENGSTROM

1

WELCOME TO THE REST OF YOUR LIFE

If a man lives many years,
let him rejoice in them all.

Congratulations. The best time of your life is here. This isn't merely your most important journey; it is your *only* journey.

Retirement changes things a bit. One man my age made these observations, which I keep in my Eclectic Notebook:

Everything is farther away than it used to be. It is twice as far to the corner and I've noticed they have added a hill.

I have given up running to catch the bus. It leaves faster than it used to, and it seems to me they are making their steps a bit steeper.

Have you noticed the smaller print they're using in the newspapers? And there is no sense in asking people to read aloud . . . everyone speaks in such a low voice I can hardly hear them.

The material they are using to make clothes is so skimpy these days, especially around the hips and waist. What they use for the length seems to be better quality.

I think my legs are getting longer, however. At times it is almost impossible to reach my shoelaces.

Even people are changing! They are much younger than they used to be when I was their age. On the other hand, people my age are much older than they used to be.

You know something? They don't even make mirrors the way they used to, either.

GREETING THE SENIOR YEARS

Whimsy aside, retirees these days *do* face a great need to prepare well for this increasingly complex time of life. Early retirement, longer life expectancy, and rapid changes in economic conditions require us to lay careful plans for the days when we'll be dimmer in our eyes, fainter in our laughter, more fond of our cane, deeper in our sighs and more frugal of our gold.

Here are a few basic suggestions for greeting the senior years. See if they don't work for you.

Acknowledge Your Age

There is nothing to be gained by fighting the inevitable. Never pretend to be younger than you are, or wish for things that are not. Since you can't change the date of your birth, you are not responsible for your age, only for what you make of it.

Others have done amazing things in the years of their seniority. At 88, for example, John Wesley was preaching daily with eloquent power and undiminished popularity.

Benjamin Franklin invented bifocals at the age of 78.

Eamon de Valera was president of Ireland at the age of 91.

At 90, Pablo Picasso was producing drawings and engravings.

At 89, Artur Rubinstein gave one of his greatest recitals in New York's Carnegie Hall.

"Grandma Moses . . . created her most famous work, Christmas Eve, *when she was 101."*

Albert Schweitzer built a hospital in Africa and managed it until he was 89.

At 88, Michelangelo did architectural plans for the Church of Santa Maria degli Angeli.

At 83, Aleksandr Derensky wrote *Russia and History's Turning Point.*

At 82, Winston Churchill wrote *A History of English-Speaking Peoples.*

At 82, Leo Tolstoy wrote *I Cannot Be Silent.*

At 81, Johann Wolfgang von Goethe finished *Faust.*

At 88, Konrad Adenauer was still serving as chancellor of Germany.

At 84, Somerset Maugham wrote *Points of View.*

Grandma Moses began oil painting at the age of 75 and created her famous work, *Christmas Eve,* when she was 101.

J. Irvin Overholtzer organized the global ministry of Child Evangelism Fellowship after he was 60 years of age.

William E. Gladstone took up a new language when he was 70. At 83, he became the prime minister of Great Britain for the fourth time.

Four major poets who lived to be more than 80 years of age did more work in the last decade of their lives than they were able to accomplish between the ages of 20 and 30.

Winston Churchill, England's great statesman who led his country through World War II, became Prime Minister for the second time when he was 78.

Michelangelo painted his greatest work, *The Last Judgment,* when he was 86.

Johann Sebastian Bach composed some of his best music at 85.

At 120, Moses' "eyes were not dim, nor was his natural force abated" (Deuteronomy 34:7). Sarah and Abraham started a family well beyond child-bearing years. Joshua and Caleb led the Hebrew army across the Jordan to conquer the Promised Land when they were in their eighties.

How old are you? Thank God for every year of experience and press on. Need and struggle are what excite and inspire us. And that's true in retirement years as well.

Don't Be Afraid to Fail

I once thought that initiative, talent, and connections were the ingredients of success. Now I believe that, paradoxically, it is an ability to fail that makes a person successful in the end. I've seen musicians, business executives, farmers, and writers fail again and again, only to press on anyhow and achieve success in the end. Just because you can't do *everything* you want in retirement, my late friend Bob Pierce would say, don't fail to do *something.* Your life is not over in retirement; it's just beginning in a new and exciting way. Strong people make mistakes as often as weak people do. The difference is that strong people admit them, laugh at them, learn from them, and press on. That is how they become strong.

> Admire those who attempt great things,
> even though they fail.
>
> Seneca

"Failure never hurt anybody," Jack Lemmon once said. "It's the fear of failure that kills you." Former California senator and author S. I. Hayakawa believed that "there is a vast difference between saying 'I have failed three times' and saying 'I am a failure.'"

Investigate New Careers

Life is a process of change. This applies both to the body we live in and to the activities we carry out at work, at play, and in worship. Work that is well chosen can add structure and pleasure to your life. It can offer stimulation and challenge and widen your social circle.

The American Association of Retired Persons (AARP) found in a survey that large numbers of older Americans prefer to continue in some form of employment after they retire. Of those people already retired, more than one-third said they would rather work than be idle. Of those over age fifty-five who are still working, about three-fourths said they would prefer to continue working even if they could afford to retire. In later chapters, this book will list some of the opportunities for fulfilling work available to senior citizens.

J. Allan Peterson, founder of *Family Concern*, underscores the wisdom of cutting back gradually by those who are heavily in demand for speaking and counseling. "It's always better to slow down voluntarily and purposefully while the invitations are still coming," he says, "rather than to wait until opportunities dry up completely and no one wants you anymore. A person nearing retirement must be proactive rather than reactive."

A pastor who built a large church thought he would be there until he retired. But he miscalculated. Because of some unforeseen problems he was asked to leave. Today he struggles with rejection, resentment, loss of ministry opportunities, a forced, premature retirement and scaled-down living accommodations.

When Dwight Swanson retired, he and his wife Audrey took a leisurely month-long vacation. At the end of that time, they stopped in Hershey, Pennsylvania, where Dwight was scheduled to address a utilities stockholders' meeting.

In the hotel lobby they noticed that a musical group was rehearsing for a Campus Crusade seminar and dinner in the same facility that evening. Because they had contributed to the ministry in the past, they decided to attend the seminar after Dwight addressed the stockholders. At the end of the Campus Crusade meeting, they joined a reception line to greet Bill and Vonette Bright, the founders of the organization.

When Bill learned that Dwight had just retired, he exclaimed, "God has sent you! I've been praying for retired businessmen to provide our ministry with professional administrative help."

Although Dwight wasn't looking for weighty responsibilities, he and Audrey visited Arrowhead Springs in San Bernardino, California, and shortly afterward entered joyfully into a whole new career. Dwight soon became heavily involved in the work as administrative associate and later as vice president of administration. Audrey became a member of the Campus Crusade Wives' Advisory Board. She also worked with the Clothes Closet, a program to help Crusade staff who faced financial crises or who were returning from overseas missions and needed clothing. She was also active as prayer coordinator for Associates in Media, a Campus Crusade ministry in Hollywood.[1]

TESTIMONIALS

To questions about how their retirement is working out, my friends have answered in many different ways. Richard C. Halverson, chaplain of the United States Senate, views retirement as an excellent time to record memories for posterity.

"Though such a record might not be publishable," he said, "it would be of great benefit to children and grandchildren."

Retirement has often failed, Stephen Lazarian told me, because retirees have mentally and physically "ceased from their labors." Steve, head of Crown City Construction Company in Pasadena, California, said he has known people who

---

> ### "People who fail in retirement . . . are those who made a living instead of making a life" (Warren W. Wiersbe).

---

have been unable to grasp the opportunities, potential, and joy of sharing the gifts that God has given them during their years of growing, learning, maturing, and mastering their calling.

Warren W. Wiersbe, former director of the "Back to the Bible Broadcast" in Lincoln, Nebraska, stressed the joy of freedom—not from responsibility or accountability, but from the shackles of schedules and pressures. "People who fail in retirement," he said, "are those who made a living instead of making a life."

To Dave Breese, head of Christian Destiny in Hillsboro, Kansas, retirement means *maturity*, which brings responsibility to pass on lessons we have learned to those who are still seeking answers.

Robert Walker, founder of Christian Life Missions and *Christian Life* magazine, sees no need to retire if a person is doing what he likes to do and can stay with it. But if forced to retire, "immediately find something else in which to serve the Lord and honor Him."

"Retirement is changing to a new chapter of life," notes Robert Andringa, president of CEO Services Group in Englewood, Colorado. Bob doesn't plan to retire as his father and father-in-law have done—by just suddenly stopping work for someone. He plans to develop relationships that will "allow [him] to continue similar activities, but on a gradually declining basis in terms of time and intensity."

For Assistant Police Chief Robert Vernon in Los Angeles, retirement will mean a shift from taking and participating to that of giving and helping. Perhaps he may spend fewer days in the trenches and more from the sidelines praying, counseling, and writing; but he wants to be somehow involved in the battle. He will prepare, he said, just as he prepared for his career in his teens by asking: (1) What do I enjoy doing? (2) What skills do people who know me well say I perform with excellence? and (3) what opportunities are becoming available?

Sociologist Tony Campolo at Eastern College in St. Davids, Pennsylvania, has studied the subject in depth.

Sociologists point out that, because of longevity, it is possible for people to have several careers in one lifetime. The first career is that of a parent who provides for the care of children as a primary vocation. The second stage, which usually begins at about 40, enables the husband and wife to become adult leaders in church and community while still carrying on gainful employment. The third career is that of formal full-time Christian service or community service that follows being released from the burden of everyday money earning.

Recently in Singapore some social scientists told me that the biggest problem of the American society is not our teenagers but our elderly people. They let me know in no uncertain terms that they felt the American population had an irresponsible elderly group. In Singapore and in China, the elderly care for the young and are engaged in helping young people through difficult times, whereas in America the elderly have a tendency to retreat from family obligations and go off to live the life of ease.

Remember what Jesus said about the man who filled his barn with the goods essential for old age security and then said, "Take ease, my soul"? The Lord said, "Thou fool . . . " (Luke 12:20).

My friend Evon Hedley notes the importance of planning in advance for these golden years and maintaining balance. "Learn," he says, "from the experience of others and be positive, always."

Wesley L. Duewell, retired president of OMS International, Greenwood, Indiana, believes that there may be a proper time to retire from administrative leadership and from some forms of involvement, but "there is never a time to retire from the principles of the stewardship of life, and Christian life is stewardship."

Visit the home of retired Methodist minister R. Hylton Saunders and his wife Dorothy in Fallbrook, California, and you'll come away inspired. Their ordered lives spent as lay counselors, the visits from their friends, the flowers in their ample garden—all speak of good preparation for their senior years. "Beauty outlasts ugliness, growth exceeds decay," says Hylt. "Almighty love is at the helm."

THE GLOW OF SUNSET

At 86, Rosie and I live by the rules of the elderly. If the toothbrush is wet, you have cleaned your teeth. If the bedside radio is warm in the morning you left it on all night. If you are wearing one brown and one black shoe, quite possibly you have a like pair in the closet.

Rosie has aged some in the past year, and now seems like a woman entering her forties. She deplores with me the miscreant who regularly enters our house in the middle of the night, squeezes the toothpaste tube in the middle, and departs.

As for me, I am as bright as can be expected, remembering the friend who told me years ago, "If your I.Q. ever breaks 100, sell!"

Like most elderly people, we spend happy hours in front of our TV set. We rarely turn it on, of course.

I walk with a slight straddle, hoping people will think I just got off a horse. I considered carrying a riding crop but gave it up—too ostentatious.

I stagger when I walk and small boys follow me, making bets on which way I'll go next. This upsets me; children shouldn't gamble.

On my daily excursions, I greet everyone punctiliously, including the headrests in parked, empty cars. Dignified friends seem surprised when I salute them with a breezy "Hi!" They don't realize I haven't enough breath for some huge two-syllable word of greeting.

My motto this year is from the Spanish: "I don't want the cheese, I just want to get out of this trap."

When we are old, the young are kinder to us, and we are kinder to each other. There is a sunset glow that irradiates our faces, and is reflected on the faces of those around us. But it is still sunset. (The late Bruce Bliven)

2

EXERCISING YOUR OPTIONS

Refuse the evil, and choose the good.

ISAIAH 7:15

You don't have to live in a senior citizens' resort to be supremely happy and well cared for in the years of your retirement. Many other options for housing, employment, and leisure are available. Study those options carefully and never move forward without careful planning and advice from many quarters.

The lifestyle we select reflects our needs and preferences and also how we view the needs of other people in our community. Lifestyle involves the use of all of our resources—time, space, and money. It develops over many years, although we seldom stand back and view it objectively.

TURTLES AND HARES

Two kinds of people prepare for retirement—turtles and hares. Turtles plan too hard, pinching and scraping for years while alienating children and living on the ragged edge just so they'll have something for retirement; hares live carelessly, spending with abandon and ending up with insufficient funds for the years when earning power is depleted.

Brad and Joanne were turtles. They had a problem with rigidity. Brad had grown up in a home with never enough money, even for basics. His dad died at age fifty, leaving his family virtually destitute. Brad began working at sixteen to support his mother and siblings. Eventually he became quite successful selling computers. For fear of being poor again, Brad forced his wife and children to live on a small fraction of his annual earnings while he invested the rest.

Brad's theme song was an adaptation of Will M. Carleton's long and mournful poem, *Over the Hill to the Poor-House*.

> Over the hill to the poor-house
>   I'm trudgin' my weary way—
> I, a man of sixty,
>   and only a trifle gray—
> I, who am smart and chipper,
>   for all the years I've told,
> As many another workman
>   that's only half as old.

Joanne was quite frustrated by Brad's austere lifestyle. Her clothing allowance was minimal; they took few vacations; they never attended sporting events even though, after thirty years of hard work, they had accumulated nearly a quarter of a million dollars. Brad had planned for the future out of fear, not faith. The lifestyle this couple developed in forty years of marriage will not likely be broken in the new schedule called retirement.

Harvey and Ann Marie, on the other hand, were hares. They seldom thought of retirement. They were generous toward their children, enjoyed lengthy vacations, followed sports with passion, but had no budget to monitor their expenditures. Their theme song was written by John Heywood in "Be Merry, Friends":

> Let the world slide, let the world go;
> A fig for care, and a fig for woe!
> If I can't pay, why, I can owe,
> And death makes equal the high and low.

Harvey and Ann Marie entered into their retirement quite differently from Brad and Joanne. Their income consisted only of their earnings from Social Security plus a small inheritance left by Ann Marie's parents. They had to adjust their lifestyle downward, causing tension in the home and not a few grumbles about how life had dealt them a poor hand. For want of planning, retirement was less than it might have been.

Solomon described Brad and Joanne in Ecclesiastes 5:13: "I have seen a grievous evil under the sun: wealth hoarded to the harm of its owner." But he also wrote about Harvey and Ann Marie: "Wealth and possessions and power to enjoy them—this is the gift of God" (v. 19). As in anything, a good thing can be carried to excess.

Many passages of Scripture commend the prudent person of industry. Proverbs 6:6–8 gives the example of the ant.

> Go to the ant, you sluggard;
> consider its ways and be wise!
> It has no commander,
> no overseer or ruler,
> yet it stores its provisions in summer
> and gathers its food at harvest.

The harvest years for most of us are between ages twenty-five and sixty. Therefore, it is wise to lay aside some of the surplus for the latter phase of our lives, when our earning abilities decline, so that we don't become a burden to our children. If you are not yet retired, take stock of your situation as follows:

- List your strengths and weaknesses honestly.

- Write down what you expect of retirement.

- Ask retired people what to expect.

- Learn about educational, recreational, social, and volunteer opportunites for retired people in your area.

- Develop support systems to replace those in your employment.

HOUSING OPTIONS

Where a retired person lives has an enormous impact both on the retirees and on their family members. Children, too, are affected by where grandpa and grandma live.

Sometimes a child's perception of those facilities is pretty amusing. I've heard many such stories about children from my friend Art Linkletter. The following school report by a child following a visit to his grandparents' mobile home park in Florida is one of my favorites.

We always spend Christmas with Grandpa and Grandma. They used to live up here in a big brick house, but Grandpa got retarded and they moved to Florida.

They live in a place with a lot of retarded people. They live in tin huts. They ride big three-wheel tricycles. They go to a big building they call the wrecked hall. But if it is a wrecked hall, it is fixed now. They play games there and do exercises, but they don't do them very good. There is a swimming pool and they go to it and just stand there in the water with their hats on. I guess they don't know how to swim. My Grandma used to bake cookies and stuff. But I guess she forgot how. Nobody cooks—they all go to fast food restaurants.

As you come into the park there is a doll house with a man sitting in it. He watches all day, so they can't get out without him seeing them. They wear badges with their names on them. I guess they don't know who they are.

My Grandma says Grandpa worked hard all his life and earned his retardment. I wish they would move back home. But I guess the man in the doll house won't let them out.

You probably will never be locked in your house by a

"Where a retired person lives has an enormous impact both on the retirees and on their family members."

---

guard in a doll house or live in a tin hut, but this is an opportunity to take another look at your living quarters. Do they suit your needs today? How will they suit you in the first years of retirement? Will you be able to handle the upkeep of the yard, pay the taxes and insurance, and negotiate its stairs and general layout?

What about your neighborhood and community? Can they accommodate your needs when you retire? Do most of your friends, family, children, grandchildren, and other relatives still live nearby? Are you satisfied with the cultural, worship, and recreational facilities nearby?

Here are some other considerations in planning your retirement housing.

- Take inventory of your current lifestyle.

- Decide whether you should move or stay where you are.

- Consider using your present quarters in creative ways.

- Study housing alternatives for elderly parents.

The thought of relocating adds intrigue to plans for retirement, but most people stay right where they've lived for most of their lives. The elderly are less likely to change residence than other age groups. In 1985, only 16 percent of persons sixty-five and older had moved since 1980 (compared with 45 percent of persons under sixty-five). The majority (80 percent) had moved to another home in the same state.

In 1985, about half (49 percent) of persons sixty-five and older lived in eight states. California, New York, and Florida had more than two million each; Illinois, Michigan, Ohio, Pennsylvania, and Texas each had more than one million.

If you follow the example of the preceding generation and choose not to relocate, your interest will focus on your current housing and nearby alternatives. You will want to know the financial and legal aspects of retirement housing, especially your present home and the money you have tied up in it if you are an owner. This section explores (a) what you know now about how you want to live and (b) how planning can make your desired lifestyle a reality.

If you decide to stay put, several steps can ease your financial concerns: Conserve heat and maintenance costs by shutting off rooms or even entire floors when they are not in use. If local statutes permit, rent out rooms for added income and perhaps companionship as well. Consider also the option of converting part of your home into an accessory apartment—an independent living unit added to, or carved out of, a single-family house. Zoning regulations in some single-family-home neighborhoods make accessory apartments illegal. But restrictions on this type of unit are being relaxed. Check with your zoning board on the legal status of accessory apartments in your community.

You can arrange for shared housing, a less structured concept than renting, in which you share your entire home with other unrelated persons, of your own age group or a mix of age groups. Check local zoning statutes first.

Your housing choice says a lot about what you can afford, whether you want privacy or closeness to neighbors, indoor or outdoor living, complete independence or complete security, formal or informal entertaining, and whether you need space for house guests, pets, elaborate hobbies, an office or study in the home.

An important feature in selecting where you live is accessibility to various facilities and services. How important are educational, medical, social, cultural, recreational, and employment opportunities in your retirement lifestyle?

Three stages of living characterize most people who are facing retirement: the *active* stage (working and taking care of yourself and your home); the *slowdown* stage (no full time work, but you still take care of your own daily needs); and finally the *dependent* stage in which you need regular medical care. Think about these stages as you plan for retirement.

Property Tax Relief

All fifty states and the District of Columbia provide some form of property tax relief to older people. The programs fall into four categories:

Circuit-breaker. This program is designed to protect family income from property tax overload. Relief usually takes the form of a direct reduction in the property tax, a refundable credit against income tax, or a cash refund.

Homestead exemption. This opportunity usually offers a fixed percentage reduction in the assessed valuation of the home or a fixed reduction in the tax bill.

Tax freeze. This proviso holds constant the tax rate existing at the time the applicant reaches a legislated age—usually sixty-three or sixty-five.

Tax deferral. This fourth initiative offers a deferral of all or part of the tax bill until the house is sold or the owner dies. The deferral is secured by a lien.

Find out what programs are available in your area. Get in touch with your state's office of taxation. In addition, the Department of Housing and Urban Development (HUD) provides some assistance to low-and moderate-income older persons who are renters. Write or phone your HUD regional or field office for current information on these federal government-assisted housing programs.

Cashing in Home Equity

Equity is the cash value of your property minus any claims against it. If your house is appraised at $120,000 and the balance due on your mortgage is $20,000, your equity is $100,000.

You can convert your equity to cash in several ways: (a) reverse mortgage, (b) sale/leaseback, or life tenancy, (c) deferred payment loan, and (d) a homeowner equity account.

Beware: Any of these financial arrangements can endanger your financial resources if not understood. Seek legal advice before signing any papers.

A *reverse mortgage* is the opposite of a conventional mortgage loan. The loan is paid to the homeowner in monthly payments, with the amount determined by the amount of home equity borrowed against, the interest rate, and the length of the loan. The loan is repaid at a scheduled time or, under certain arrangements, when the homeowner dies or sells the home. In some cases, the home must be sold to settle the obligation.

A *sale/leaseback*, or *life tenancy*, provision allows the owner to sell the property, often at below-market rate, to an investor. The owner retains the right to live in the house for life as a renter. The investor pays the owner in monthly installments over a period agreed upon and also covers the obligations of home ownership such as insurance, taxes, and repairs. Quite often deferred-payment annuity is purchased at the outset to provide the owner with continued monthly income once the house has been paid off by the investor.

A *deferred-payment loan* allows older homeowners to draw upon home equity to maintain and repair the property. This holds property value high. This kind of loan is often provided by a local government for low-income persons at a low interest rate. It allows homeowners to defer payment of all principal and interest until the homeowner dies or the house is sold.

Homeowner equity accounts are available from brokerage houses and banks nationwide. This option allows the homeowner to set up a line of credit secured by a lien against his or her house. The maximum amount would equal 70 percent of the equity accumulated in the house. The homeowner can draw on this line of credit by using a credit card or by writing a check to buy anything at all except stocks. However, loans must be repaid with interest over a specified time that begins when the loan is secured. Payments are not deferred.

Before making any move, obtain good legal counsel. Make certain that you understand all that is involved in each program and what the ramifications might be.

COOPERATIVE HOUSING

Condominium, cooperative, or life care residences are popular with senior citizens. Before making any purchases or signing any long-term contract for housing, of course, get legal advice.

Are costs subject to an increase? If a monthly fee is required for maintenance or services, find out if the fee is subject to an increase and how rates may be raised.

Who pays for recreation? The facility may offer a swimming pool, golf course, and game room and then after you move in, turn over the operating costs of these wonderful assets to the residents. If the contract so specifies, you might find yourself paying much more for their use than you thought. These amenities do improve the salability of the property, however.

What are your rights and restrictions? The fine print in your housing agreement may place restrictions on visitors, entertaining, or ownership of pets. You may also find that there are restrictions on how and to whom you can sell your property.

If you are a tenant in a building that may be converted into a condominium, you will need to know what your legal rights and obligations will be in such a conversion. State and local laws vary widely, but most give tenants the right of first refusal. And in some states older persons are given certain protections, such as being able to retain their unit on a rental basis if the building goes condo. Since conversion can be a complicated matter, tenants opposed to it should organize and should retain a lawyer or get other expert opinion.

Tenants should also be aware of any local rent-control ordinances that apply in their circumstances. If a landlord violates a rent-control ordinance, the tenant must take his or her own steps to rectify the matter. No one else will do it for the tenant.

Time-sharing arrangements for vacation or other part-time housing require careful investigation as well. The concept of time sharing is sound, but the industry is poorly regulated.

WORK OPTIONS

The American Association of Retired Persons (AARP) has found through surveys that many older people want to work, but not full time. Whatever you decide about work, ideally it should be *your* decision, not one that is forced upon you.

Study these alternatives now so that you will be ready when the time comes.

Tapering-off Programs. Occasionally employers provide the alternative of phased retirement to their employees. By working progressively shorter hours and taking longer vacations, employees can adjust gradually to the increased amount of retirement leisure time.

Flextime. Variable work hours and employees on one job are popular. With flextime, companies find that workers' job satisfaction and performance improve.

Part-time work. In many parts of the country, older workers can find part-time employment after they retire from a regular job. Part-time work offers extra income and personal satisfaction. In some areas, placement agencies exist specifically to make job matches between older workers and local employers.

Retraining or Re-entry. Some companies have programs to retrain employees for less demanding jobs. Occasionally these companies rehire workers to serve in various capacities; for example, part time at their old job or temporarily in seasonal jobs.

A New Career. It can be refreshing to begin a totally new career in middle or later life. Some retirees start their own businesses centering around their hobbies or interests.

Voluntarism. I am devoting an entire chapter to this subject a bit later. Through volunteer work, the world is at your feet. Many agencies have work ready and waiting. Some pay expenses. Others work through churches and/or all sorts of group participation.

CASE STUDIES

Let me share examples of some actual cases. How would you solve the problems these people face?

Pre-Retirement Blues

Mark Fisher is employed as a salesman for a large title company. He fears retirement, which is just three years away. He feels depressed and dragged out at the end of the day. Which of the following suggestions do you think would work the best?

1. Mark can get a physical examination.
   (How can illness affect mental attitudes and vice versa?)

2. He can ask the company's personnel department for help.
   (In what ways could the personnel department help?)

3. He can ignore retirement and try not to think about it.
   (What could happen if he attempts to forget the future?)

4. He can start making positive plans for retirement.
   (What will this shift do for Mark?)

5. Other options:

For Better or for Worse, but for Lunch, Too?

Susan McIntire dreads the day her husband retires and stays home all day long. She pictures her husband underfoot, interfering with her tight schedule of activities in her home, church, and community. What should she do?

1. Susan can plan individual and shared activities with her husband, starting now. (How would this help? What activities would you suggest?)

2. She can suggest that her husband find part-time work. (How might her husband respond to this suggestion?)

3. She can plan ways to guarantee privacy in the home for each family member. (But if the quarters are small, how would this be arranged?)

4. She can suggest swapping chores for added interest. (What are some of the chores that could be exchanged?)

5. Other options:

Mike's Bike Shop

Michael Purvis can fix anything. Neighbors bring him their clocks, cars, flat tires, and toys; and somehow he manages somehow to patch them all up. He has been doing this work in his basement and wants to branch out into a small bike shop when he retires in three years. What should Mike do now?

1. Establish his business now and retire when the shop is going well? (How could Michael operate his own shop and still work until retirement?)

2. Cancel plans to open a shop. Too much work without enough profit. (What risk is there in this move? What else could he try?)

3. Set up his business now to have it operating by the time his retirement takes effect. (What all is involved in setting up a business? Would it be better to complete all planning for the new enterprise before retirement?)

4. Quit work now and go into business right away. (What is there to be gained? Why might it be better to keep working at his regular job?)

5. Other options:

Preparing for the Big Day

In four years, Randall Jones will retire; but he doesn't see how he and his wife can live on their retirement income. What can he do now to test his retirement resources?

1. Begin now to live on a reduced income. (Would a budget help? In what ways might he reduce his expenses?)

2. Take early retirement and get going. (What are some steps he could take to plan well?)

3. Find a part-time job or organize a small business. (What are some of the benefits of a part-time job or a small business in retirement years?)

4. Find a less expensive retirement area. (In what ways could Randall pre-test an area? What sort of characteristics might he look for in such an area?)

5. Other options:

A Missionary Comes Home

Eleanore Price spent most of her life overseas in missionary work caring for others. Now she plans to retire, but she discovers that she hardly knows herself. What steps can Eleanore take to build up her self-esteem and prepare for living alone?

1. Ask her family members, because they know her best. (Are they in a position to advise? Would they put her needs first?)

2. Meditate, attend church, see her pastor. (What other agencies, people, and organizations are available? What should she do if these are of no help?)

3. Learn to enjoy solitude and to relax—physically, mentally, and spiritually—and enjoy her individual-

ity. (How could Eleanore take steps to reach this situation?)

4. Join a prayer group, singing ensemble, and craft workshop for fellowship and nurturing. (How could these groups help Eleanore? What good things could come of these associations?)

5. Other options:

"To retire earlier than age sixty-five, Harvard found, significantly lowered one's longevity."

DEMOGRAPHICS

Increased life expectancy has caused the population of America to grow rapidly. In 1982, approximately two out of every ten United States citizens were fifty-five or older; by the year 2030, the United States Census Bureau predicts that this figure will be slightly more than three in ten. By 2050 more than 5 percent of the population will be eighty-five or older.

Retirement doesn't automatically provide better health, a stronger marriage, and freedom from worry. A study sponsored by Harvard University involving graduates who had reached the age of seventy-five surprised the pollsters. Among one hundred men who had retired at age sixty-five, seven of eight were dead by the age of seventy-five. And to retire earlier, Harvard found, significantly lowered one's longevity.

Gerontologists see ahead a growing number of vital, well-educated, financially secure retirees who will demand a greater voice in national policy making decisions. What an enormous resource this group will provide to the country!

IT'S ABOUT TIME

For everything there is a season,
and a time for every matter under heaven.

ECCLESIASTES 3:1

*T*ime, a phenomenon often regarded as the foe of man's dominion, is actually the friend of us senior citizens. "Touch us gently, time," wrote Barry Cornwall in *A Petition to Time* long ago. "Let us glide down thy stream gently. . . ."

"Write it on your heart," Ralph Waldo Emerson said even at the peak of the Civil War, "that every day is the best day of the year."[1] And it was Oliver Wendell Holmes who observed while sitting as a justice on the United States Supreme Court that "time keeps its customers in arrears by lending them minutes and charging them years."

During most of our working years, supervisors, managers, and efficiency experts constantly reminded us that time is money. They meant, of course, that workers should carry out their assignments with more efficiency so that the company might profit. But now in the new over sixty-five generation, we can rephrase that to read, Time is more precious than money. Now we spend our time as carefully as we ever did our money during wage-earning years. As we grow older, there is less and less time in our bank accounts.

What, precisely, is time? Who can explain it? What do we talk more about than time? St. Augustine thought he could

---

"As we grow older, there is less and less time in our bank accounts."

---

explain time until he was asked. Then he replied, "If nobody asks me, then I know. But if I were desirous to explain to someone that should ask me, plainly I know not."

A group of experienced news commentators was once asked at year's end to identify the gravest crisis facing the American people. Eric Sevareid, for many years a CBS commentator, cited the rise of leisure and the fact that those who have the most leisure are the least equipped to make use of it.[2]

For a retired person, leisure can mean tedious boredom. Once upon a time, our busy work schedules added tension to our lives; now the opposite is true. How can we spend our leisure time redemptively? Leisure time should include things we *want* to do but don't *have* to do.

Each day contains twenty-four hours, but each person uses those hours in different ways. People have always been puzzled by this phenomenon called time. What is it? How should we spend it? Henry Dobson in "The Paradox of Time" alluded to its intriguing essence:

Time goes, you say? Ah, no!
Alas, Time stays, we go.[3]

Time that is measured fights against time that is lived. Each person has an equal amount. Whether school boy or president, author or housewife, farmer or financier, the clocks we buy all run at the same rate of speed. No one has a single second more of time than anyone else.

I like Charles Shedd's "Ten Affirmations for Christian Use of Time."[4] He begins with the purpose of time: Life's Single Holy Assignment. From Luke 10:41-42 he sets forth the parallel of Christ's reminder to Martha that "one thing is needful." The Savior recommended a simple, quiet talk about heavenly things over bending her efforts toward lavish attentions. The effective life, writes Pastor Shedd, does not result from getting God to help us. Our lives assume maximum worth when we "turn our wills over to Him and ask that we might be of assistance to His purposes."

When life becomes too harried, Colleen Townsend Evans says she tries to stop the merry-go-round with the question, "Have I pushed Christ out of the center of my life?"[5]

Pastor and writer Bruce Larson suggests that "getting our marching orders can make the difference."[6] Settling the question of whether what we are doing is what *God wants* us to be doing could be the greatest single key to our management of time!

Take away the complicated phrases and we must conclude that time is but a measurement, a dimension. Therefore, time need not be a problem for someone who is retired and has plenty of it. All roads lead right back to a management, not of time, but of ourselves.

DEALING WITH LEISURE

The psalmist uses the term *selah* to indicate a pause in the reading of the psalter while music plays. Music uses a symbol called a rest at certain locations on the score. There is no music in the rest but, as John Ruskin pointed out, "there's the making of music in it." Retired persons are in a good position to take advantage of that rest to make their lives a symphony.

God introduced leisure when He created the world in six days and rested on the seventh. What do you think of when you think of leisure time? A quiet stroll on the beach; a thiry-foot Air Stream trailer behind your car as you travel to the North Woods? Playing croquet in the back yard? Warming your toes beside your fireplace on a cold winter night?

The term *leisure* comes from the Latin *licere,* meaning to be permitted. We will not experience leisure until we give ourselves permission. Do you think that is an odd thing to say? Who *wouldn't* give himself permission to enjoy a bit of leisure? I'll tell you who: every workaholic you meet (I wrote a book on that subject); every frazzled wife trying to cope with a retired husband underfoot; every single parent holding a job and a family together; and every guilt-ridden provider who frets against having so little saved for retirement and pours his energies into several jobs.

Leisure is not unwork. It's not whittling wood, twiddling thumbs, or watching the sun rise and then set again. Leisure here refers to meaningful work for which we were made. This generation has robbed leisure of its balm. The young executive is told, "You want to get ahead here? Work overtime. Work fifteen-hour days and travel on Sundays."

How will a person ever get to know God with a schedule like that? Most middle class Americans tend to worship their work. They work at their play and play at their worship. Meaningful values are thus distorted; relationships disintegrate; lifestyle becomes a cast of characters in search of a plot.

William McNamara states that our neurotic compulsion to work is our country's greatest malaise. To Tim Hansel, even work that is good and necessary can become idolatry when it becomes all-consuming.

Handling leisure requires the same discipline as handling any part of one's time. Mark H. McCormack learned over the years how to arrange his schedule to accommodate his work habits. "For me," he said, "getting the most out of my abilities is directly proportionate to getting the most out of my time. I take an aggressive attitude toward time, and I seek to control it rather than have it control me."[7]

There are four ways to fill the hours of retirement.

1. "I'll wait until I wake up each morning to plan the new day."

2. "I don't merely want to keep busy; I want to *enjoy* the things I do. So I will plan to spend a maximum of time for the things I like and a minimum of time for those activities which I do not enjoy."

"We will not experience leisure until we give ourselves permission."

---

3. "It isn't enough merely to enjoy myself; I want to have some meaning to my life. I want my activities to furnish that meaning."

4. "What does it matter if I enjoy myself? I must spend and be spent by my mission. In this passion I find meaning."

Which one describes the way you fill the time of your life?

The first one can be deadly. Marlene Alexander of Newmarket, Ontario, said after her father died one autumn at eighty-four years of age that "we watched Dad die by degrees ever since he quit work when he was sixty-five."

The thing that worried me was that he didn't retire *to* anything. At the time, my parents had a big house with a big yard and a vegetable garden, but they soon sold the property and moved into a condominium.

For as long as I can remember, Dad had always enjoyed going for long walks. Somewhere along the way he stopped doing that or anything else very active. Then, at 75, we discovered that he was diabetic. Mom prepared his meals according to the strict diet, but he craved sweets. (Why is it we always long for those things that are bad for us?) Any walks he took now led to the nearest store where he could get candy and ice cream. Nobody could make him understand the seriousness of his actions. It seemed as though eating was the only pleasure left to him. Eventually, he lost what remained of his already poor eyesight and a stroke immobilized him for about a year before he died.

In her 23 February 1991 column, Ann Landers published this humorous but insightful prayer by a senior citizen.

A Prayer for Later Years

Lord, Thou knowest that I am growing older.

Keep me from becoming too talkative, and particularly keep me from falling into the tiresome habit of expressing an opinion on every subject.

Release me from the craving to straighten out everybody's affairs. Keep my mind free from the recital of endless details. Give me wings to get to the point.

Give me grace, dear Lord, to listen to others describe their aches and pains. Help me endure the boredom with patience and to keep my lips sealed, for my own aches and pains are increasing in number and intensity and the pleasure of discussing them is becoming sweeter as the years go by.

Teach me the glorious lesson that, occasionally, I might be mistaken. Keep me reasonably sweet. I do not wish to be a saint (saints are so hard to live with) but a sour old person is the work of the devil.

Make me thoughtful, but not moody; helpful, but not pushy; independent, yet able to accept with graciousness favors that others wish to bestow on me.

Free me of the notion that simply because I have lived a long time I am wiser than those who have not lived so long.

If I do not approve of some of the changes that have taken place in recent years, give me the wisdom to keep my mouth shut.

Lord knows that when the end comes, I would like to have a friend or two left.

Senior C

A woman in upstate New York ran her home in her retirement precisely as she had during the busy haunts of the work-a-day world. Only when she broke her ankle did she find that life went on without washday on Monday, grocery shopping on Wednesday, and tennis on Saturday. The revelation changed her life and made her much easier to live with.

In spending your time, don't count on everything going as planned. How dull a life it would be if everything happened as anticipated! How wonderful to know that God can take our mistakes and work them out for good.

Looking back, Joseph could have taken comfort in Murphy's law: If anything can go wrong, it probably will. His brothers sold him as a slave to Egyptians. His master's wife tried to seduce him, leading to an unjust sentence. Those he befriended in prison forgot him. But when it was all over, Joseph could say to his brothers, "You meant it for evil, but the Lord meant it for good."

My colleague Ed Dayton at World Vision, and my partner in our two-day "Managing Your Time" seminars for pastors and Christian leaders, has created a new law which he calls Dayton's Law: At least 50 percent of the things you plan will probably go right. Rejoice!

That goes especially for retirement. God never gives us more than we can handle. Other people will, however. And we assign ourselves an overload, but the Lord never does. Charles W. Shedd, in his book *Time For All Things*, writes:

> God knows what He wants from each of us, and there is plenty of time in His day for things essential to His plan. We do Him a grave injustice when we fall into the habit of compulsive overwork. We sin when we pressure out His wishes for assignments that have not been filtered through divine judgment. Self-centered scheduling that wants it our way, and ours alone, is far different from setting up a plan with the Inner Presence as our guide.[8]

Dwight D. Eisenhower arranged his affairs so that only the truly important and urgent matters came across his desk. He discovered in the process that the two seldom went together. The really important matters were seldom urgent . . . and the most urgent matters were seldom important.

Too much of a set schedule can become an idol, says Michael Griffiths in *Take My Life*. "If we get irritated when something comes along to interfere with it."[9] There is great joy, he pointed out, in meeting calm, unhurried people, who in spite of their own pressures still have time for others. Some people have the temperament to be organized and prepared, rather than to be in a rush. The rest of us have to work at it. Better to be serene and to cultivate an unhurried life.

The Institute of Gerontology at the University of Michigan surveyed senior citizens about their formulas for remaining active, useful, and happy in retirement. The respondents answered:

- Doing busy work isn't enough; neither is a hobby.

- Plan some activities with other people.

- Continue learning, regardless of your age.

- Stay in touch with younger people.

- Do something for someone else at least once a day.

- Try out your activities before retirement.

WHAT SHALL I DO?

Whatever you choose to do during your retirement years, make certain that you choose activities with continuity, so that you can return to them again and again. And, while you may master the basic skills easily, your activities should keep you challenged. You don't want to get bored when you become an expert! Your activities need to:

- Fulfill a wide range of needs and wants.

- Lead to your growth and development.

- Improve your self-esteem.

- Satisfy the needs that work once did, and most important, give you a sense of accomplishment and creativity.

- Leave time for daily scripture reading and prayer.

An abundance of activities exist to fill your leisure hours. Here is a sampling to introduce you to kinds you might not have thought of.

Adult Education

Our types are returning to classrooms in record numbers. Adult education programs present a wide range of subjects including practical skills such as woodworking, enjoyable pastimes such as genealogy studies, and academic pursuits such as languages and literature.

Colleges and universities are seeking older students with or without high school diplomas. Special counseling programs, adult-oriented course offerings, the College Level Examination Program (which gives credit for life experience), and scholarships or subsidies for senior citizens are only a few of the ways in which these institutions are luring older people back to school. You can earn a degree just for the satisfaction of it, or prepare yourself for starting a business. You may desire to stimulate your intellect, or you may enter into a spiritual ministry for needy people all around you.

Trade schools offer job-directed training, even for retired persons. Correspondence schools administer independent study programs by mail in both credit and noncredit subjects. The doors of public libraries, museums, televised classes, learning aids, churches, and senior centers are open to us.

Elderhostel is one innovative educational program which offers liberal arts and science courses to American and Canadian citizens sixty years of age and older. The program began in 1975 as an experiment at five schools in the New Hampshire state college system. It grew out of the Institute for Retired Professionals, established in 1962. In ten years, nearly 100,000 participants had joined the sessions at a total of 850 institutions in all fifty states and in many countries abroad. Classes are supplemented with field trips and social events. The modest charge includes room and board in the institution's dormitories. If you are interested in being added to Elderhostel's mailing list, send a postcard with your name and address to:

Elderhostel Institute Network
15 Garrison Avenue
Durham, NH 03824

Older adults care about education. They are intense and self-motivated learners, and they define their own educational experiences and enthusiasms. An institute fosters and capitalizes on these strengths, empowering older people to continue learning, expand their horizons, and enhance their personal development.

Crafts and Hobbies

"No person is really happy or safe without a hobby," wrote Sir William Osler, a distinguished teacher-physician.[10] For

---

"Older adults care about education. They are intense and self-motivated learners."

---

many years I've been curious about hobbies, finding in sports my keenest interest. People choose hobbies in many ways (perhaps hobbies choose people, I'm not sure). Usually an avocation in the years before retirement becomes a second vocation in retirement. Most of the time, the hobby that seizes the interest of a retiree is a brand new experience.

Which of the following hobbies would capture your interest: auctions, autograph collecting, baking, bird watching, animals, coin collecting, drawing, painting, fishing, stamp collecting, writing, window-shopping . . . ? Izaak Walton wrote, "I have laid aside business, and gone a-fishing." And, to justify his action, he added, "We may say of angling as Dr. Boteler said of strawberries: 'Doubtless God could have made a better berry, but doubtless God never did'; and so, if I might be judge, God never did make a more calm, quiet, innocent recreation than angling."[11]

Reading is a keen hobby for me. I've read a book a week for the past forty or more years. For most of those years I read to enrich my ministry in management. Now I read for fun and inspiration as well. I have the ability to speed read most of the books I read.

In *The Haunted Bookshop*, Christopher Morley gives the old bookman a curious reason for not reading some of his favorite books. His strategy was that when it came time to die and the doctors were certain he would not recover, he would cry, "But I can't die! I haven't read *King Lear!*"

Travel is high on the list of priorities for most retired people, but it's expensive so desire is most often modified by the check book. It might be that it's more important for you to travel to the next state to see a treasured friend than it is to fly to Europe next summer.

J. Winston Pearce, writer in residence at Campbell University in Buies Creek, North Carolina, has a creative way to travel by car and cut down on expenses.

"The Pearces often travel with friends by car," he says. "And, tongue in cheek, I report on one way the four of us cut expenses. We found that the four of us, two couples, needed only one motel room with two double beds. When friends raise an eyebrow at that and ask if it is not embarrassing when we go to bed, I answer, 'No, we learned that if we took off our bifocals, there were no problems.'"[12]

The famous Roman orator Cicero once wrote, "If the soul has food for study and learning, nothing is more delightful than an old age of leisure." Cultivating the mind and heart, to be sure, is more important for one than what goes on in one's environment.

> My mind to me a kingdom is;
> Such present joys therein I find
> That it excels all other bliss
> That earth affords or grows by kind.[13]

If a retired person can settle upon a hobby that improves the mind, so much the better. After Franklin Delano Roosevelt was elected president, he called on Justice Oliver Wendell Holmes, Jr., and found the man reading Plato at the age of ninety-two. "May I ask why you are reading Plato, Mr. Justice?" asked the president.

"Certainly, Mr. President," came the reply, "to improve my mind."

It's been said often that the happiest people in retirement are those who touch life at the greatest number of points.

Woodworking, bookbinding, candlemaking, photography, ceramics, printing, quilting, upholstering, toymaking—these are only a few examples of the many crafts and hobbies people pursue. You can enjoy crafts alone or with others,

---

"The happiest people in retirement are those who touch life at the greatest number of points."

---

spend as much money and time as you like on them, fashion them for your own amusement, or give them away. You might want to teach others your crafts as well.

You can learn about crafts in adult education courses or classes at your local Y, art center, or senior center. You will find craft magazines and books in local libraries.

Gardening. Tilling soil is creative in many ways. The gardener fosters life, nurtures beauty, gains peace of mind, and becomes attuned to God's creation. Gardening can be as simple as planting a window box, or as advanced as growing plants for sale or collecting and raising rare specimens.

To gain skills in gardening:

- Talk to your gardener friends.

- Visit your library or bookstore.

- Inquire about church or senior center gardening programs.

Writing. Retirement, as United States Senate Chaplain Richard C. Halverson suggested in the opening chapter, is a good time to record the history and lineage of your family. Through writing you can express thoughts, share ideas, and free your emotions. You may even decide to send your work to a publisher.

Courses in creative writing are available in most areas at community colleges, at recreation centers, through university continuing-education programs, and by correspondence. Classes by mail for writers are easier to conduct than most other types of subjects because a student must first put his work on paper whether the instructor is right there in the class or at a remote mailbox.

Drawing, Painting, and Sculpting. The arts help us become more sensitive to the world around us and more appreciative of texture, color, and shadow. University and adult education programs, art museums, and private studios offer formal training. Older people may be entitled to reduced tuition fees.

You can borrow famous reproductions or works by community artists for your home. Special events such as book discussions, film forums, or lectures are available. So are popular and specialized newspapers and magazines.

Music. Within a period of only twelve months you could learn to play sophisticated music on a recorder, a piano, an organ, a guitar, or an accordion. Many music shops, educational institutions, and musicians offer lessons. Self-instruction is available through learn-by-mail organizations as well.

Cooking. Skill in the kitchen requires imagination more than the mastering of measurements for recipes. Many people enjoy special pleasure from inventing and/or perfecting a favorite dish.

To learn how to cook, borrow cookbooks from your library, watch a cooking series on television, take classes, or learn by trial and error.

Collecting. Accumulating items of interest can be amusing, satisfying, and financially rewarding as well. Your search might be a personal treasure hunt or a studied garnering of items you know are valuable and on which you can turn a profit.

For starters, you might collect antique furniture, rare books, buttons, bottles, cars, clocks, coins, dolls, old prints, or stamps—to name a few possibilities. Libraries, bookstores, and local and national collectors' clubs can provide information not only on the process of collecting but also on how to evaluate and sell your collections.

Reading. Reading opens your mind to a special world of thought and imagination. Reading endures despite the appeal of television, radio, and video games. Many still prefer the printed page for the pursuit of knowledge and the entertainment of a well crafted story. Certainly, reading is one of the best ways to exercise your imagination.

Physical Fitness

The results of exercise, just like those of good nutrition, are cumulative throughout a lifetime of good selection. The earlier you start pursuing physical fitness, the better off you will be. Regardless of your previous history, the cardinal rule of fitness past fifty is *movement*—ideally, the kind of movement that builds your heart and lung capacity, maintains your body flexibility, and increases your muscular strength. Walking, cycling, swimming, and other aerobic exercises can help you accomplish these goals. If this type of exercise is too ambitious for you, at least try to avoid the sedentary life as much as possible. Don't just *sit!* Physical activity stimulates the mind as well as the body. Give it priority in your schedule.

As with education, opportunities are almost limitless for older people. Competitive sports are available in most communities. Get into archery, badminton, basketball, cycling, bowling, diving, fencing, golf, horseshoes, ice skating, karate, soccer, rowing, softball, table tennis, tennis, swimming, and running, according to your preferences. Before taking the plunge, however, have a complete physical examination. Ask your doctor to recommend sports that suit your age and state of health.

Walking. No exercise is more natural than walking. It suits people of all ages. No special equipment is required, and you can walk in all kinds of weather. Start today.

Cycling. The same leg muscles used in walking are used in cycling. Cycling is more effective than walking in expanding lung capacity. Cycling is an increasingly popular sport. Investigate the types of bikes available to buy, or rent a three-, five-, or ten-speed bike. A coaster is a three-wheeled "trike." An exercycle in the home offers the same idea.

Swimming. Whether you do it for style, speed, or just plain fun, swimming is a wonderfully effective exercise. It tones the body, increases lung capacity, and aids circulation. Special swimming exercises can develop or trim specific body parts. Most areas offer swimming as a year-round sport, because many clubs and communities have indoor pools. Check on reduced rates and special lessons available to seniors.

In these recent years, swimming and golf have been my favorite forms of exercise and recreation.

Dealing with Stress. An important part of physical fitness is the management of stress. Medical researchers link stress to high blood pressure, kidney disease, ulcers and other digestive problems, and the general wearing down of the body's immune system. In addition, stress is a strong risk factor in the development of heart disease and cancer.

Allowing stress to pollute your valuable retirement time is a serious mistake, but one which you can correct. First, determine what causes your stress, and then learn to deal with it in a healthful way.

Social Activities

In addition to hobbies and physical fitness, social activities play a vital role in maintaining a happy, productive retirement.

Special Interest Organizations. Clubs help you to do more with less. They provide social encounters, windows of opportunity unavailable for a person alone, and companionship in the development of skills, pursuits of like interests, and economical group activities for enterprising retired persons. And, most churches have wonderful opportunities of this kind of fellowship.

Travel. Moving about in this big, wide, wonderful world the Lord has created for us involves more than sightseeing. It includes interacting with people in distant places. To make travel more affordable, many organizations offer special tours and discounts to retirees.

Planning for a trip is half the fun. Successful travel, like successful retirement, needs a goal. If you're a photography buff, you'll bring back images from other places to enjoy for a lifetime. Better than a camera, however, is the human memory of what you saw. Ralph Waldo Emerson wrote, "Though we travel the world over to find the beautiful, we must carry it with us or we find it not."

A single retired person can make travel more enjoyable by following these suggestions.

- Take an interest in other people and other parts of the country and other lands.

- Make some first moves; don't always wait for another person to do so.

- Choose places to go and things to do that you know you will enjoy.

- Forget the workaday world, and just be yourself.

Meditation

Enjoying contemplative activity is one of the most fruitful ways elderly people can spend time alone. In years past, you contemplated the origins of life, the world God has created, and the future of the soul. These were laid aside, most probably, as the pressures of earning a living and rearing a family distracted on all sides.

Now in later years, we can begin assessing our lives and relationships again.

If the resources of retirement years are to be well used, retirees must become masters of their own time. Time is not limitless; it is a valuable resource to spend carefully. The rewards will be yours not only for time, but for eternity as well.

An essential benefit of time well spent is enjoyment. You should enjoy what you're doing whether you're doing it for yourself or for others. To enjoy your free time to the utmost, regard it as an opportunity to look anew at yourself and your life, to come closer to the meaning of your life in relation to the world around you, to continue to grow personally, emotionally, and spiritually. Ideally, your emphasis in retirement should be on *learning* to live rather than *earning* a living.

RETIREMENT IS FOR GRANDPARENTING

One of the best ways to use your increased leisure time is to get serious about grandparenting. Happiness is being a grandparent, says a popular bumper sticker. That's true until the little shavers wear us out. Then we're happy to see their parents rescue us. But most retired people put grandparenting up there at the top of their favorite pastimes. When our own kids were small we worked most of the time, trying to become established, taking care of responsibilities at work, making sure all of the bills were paid. We were proud of our own youngsters but there wasn't time enough to enjoy them. Now the picture has changed.

I can't imagine Christmas, birthdays, and other holidays without our grandchildren. And I can't imagine not planning various activities which involve the grandchildren who, I'm happy to say, live nearby. These times, I'm sure, will have a positive influence on their lives in later years.

Childhood is changing for our grandchildren. Nowadays it's television, computer games, and videos. We grandparents must be there when they need us. Our influence can be enormous, but there are ways to win their hearts and ways to turn them away. Let's use our time to ensure that succeeding generations learn to walk in the ways of the Lord.

4

ONE FOR
YOUR MONEY

*No man is so wise that he may not
easily err if he takes no other counsel but his own.*

BEN JONSON

*D*o you know your savings account balance; your credit rating; how much money you can expect to have in retirement; whether you have enough life insurance to protect a spouse or any dependents; your net worth; how much money you spend each month; and whether your investments are appropriate in today's economy?

If you have the answers to these questions, even if they are only estimates, you are exceptionally well aware of your financial resources. Historically, women have been especially ill prepared to save, invest, and manage their money. Some are single parents struggling as widows to raise children; others are beyond their careers, facing retirement without the support of a male provider; still others are married to husbands who fancy themselves to be good financial planners and only begrudgingly share knowledge of the couple's economic situation. To all, I say don't hesitate to ask questions, to study investment opportunities, and to give attention to your resources. All too easily they slip away and are lost for a lifetime.

Business and governments continually employ a variety of consultants, yet individuals often do not take advantage even of the advice available to them at no charge through financial agencies. "In a multitude of counselors there is safety," Proverbs 11:14 reminds us. But who wants to listen to advice, especially if it flies in the face of our own guarded opinions?

The political philosopher Edmund Burke was impressed by the multiplier effect of advice: "He who calls in the aide of an equal understanding doubles his own; and he who profits by superior understanding raises his powers to a level with the heights of the superior understanding he unites with."[1] Taking advice is a delicate issue. Many a fortune has been lost through wrong advice; many friendships have ended through friendly advice that cut too close to the bone. People sometimes reject wise counsel given in the spirit of friendship. Dr. Samuel Johnson, an Englishman of nineteenth century, observed that "vanity is so frequently the apparent motive of advice that we, for the most part, summon our powers to oppose it without any very accurate inquiry whether it is right."[2]

How do you know when to accept financial advice?

All of us, I'm certain, have had friends who willingly, and far too often ignorantly, offered us financial and investment advice. I vividly recall a close colleague and friend suggesting a sure-fire financial opportunity in the purchase of a top-grade Arabian horse, or a portion thereof! The horse belonged to a seemingly successful Arabian horse ranch. I purchased a portion of an Arabian horse (I'm not quite sure which part of the anatomy it was) for several thousand dollars. (I can't miss an investment.) Not many months later a disease hit the horse ranch; and my horse, among others, went to horse heaven—and took with it my investment.

Lesson learned: be very careful what investment counsel you accept, even from well-meaning friends.

On another occasion, a very successful publishing executive friend convinced me that investing in a new 3-D project

---

"During your years of employment, income meant a paycheck. . . . That paycheck ends with retirement."

---

with Disney Productions could do nothing less than quadruple my invested funds. I bit—considerably. Not long after that, we all realized that the 3-D market had closed up, and our investment went down the drain. Why it took me so long to learn not to invest in these can't-fail new projects I'll never know. But I did learn.

Private pensions sprang up in the forties and flourished in the fifties as employers set up programs to provide financial independence and increased leisure time for employees.

Seminars and workshops designed to prepare employees for the financial and emotional adjustments of later years became popular in the fifties. Early retirement incentive packages that often seem too attractive to pass up leave many persons prematurely cut off from work, frequently with little or no preparation.

The Age Discrimination in Employment Act (ADEA) and its 1986 amendments give legal protection to most workers over the age of forty, but early retirement is becoming increasingly popular. Records of the Social Security Administration show that more workers are electing to start receiving reduced retirement benefits at ages sixty-two, sixty-three, and sixty-four rather than waiting until age sixty-five or older to collect full benefits. This trend is more noticeable among male workers than female workers.

Inflation affects retirement plans for many people. The low birthrates in the 1970s may lead to labor shortages in the 1990s; older workers may then be persuaded to stay on the job, instead of being encouraged to move out and make a place for younger employees. The growing numbers of women entering the work force will affect retirement patterns. Because female employees tend to begin working later in life than their male counterparts, they may need to remain in the work force longer than men of the same age to become vested in their pension plans.

LAYING A FINANCIAL FOUNDATION

During your years of employment, *income* meant a paycheck every week, fortnight, or month. While you kept working, the paychecks, interest, and dividends kept coming in.

That paycheck ends with retirement. Most of your income will now be derived from other sources—sources that have been building up over the years. Until now, they've remained largely untapped. No matter when your retirement begins, it is never too early or too late to begin the important planning required in order to sustain that income.

Let me suggest that you use the following outline as you plan your future, no matter where you are in your age bracket, prior to your retirement.

1. Prepare a list of your needs and desires after the paycheck stops.

2. Determine which sources of income will be relatively permanent (pension, Social Security benefits), and which will be temporary (part-time work, debts owed to you).

3. List sources of income which will keep paying after the death of the person receiving the income (spousal benefits on a pension). Will income continue after the death of a spouse who is receiving the pension benefits? Get precise figures here; don't guess at them.

4. Find out which sources of income will be stable and which will fluctuate with interest rates and the upward and downward movement of stocks and bonds. No one can predict the exact course of such investments, but make a calculated guess.

5. Ask yourself when, if ever, it might be wise to dip into your accumulated principal.

When to Tap into Your Principle

Let's say you have $10,000 invested at 7 percent, compounding quarterly. You can withdraw the following monthly amounts for the stated number of years. At the end of that time, the $10,000 will be gone:

Monthly Withdrawal	Length of Time
$116	10 years
$89	15 years
$77	20 years
$70	25 years
$59	*Indefinitely

Let's put that another way: A total of $10,000 will actually yield $21,000 if it is withdrawn over a 25-year period: $70 per month times 300 months equals $21,000. To determine monthly withdrawals based upon other sums, multiply the above figures by the number of tens of thousands of dollars in the beginning amount. For example if the beginning amount were $25,000, multiply the above figures by 2.5. On a 25-year withdrawal plan, the monthly withdrawal will be 2.5 times $70, or $175. The amount of withdrawal, of course, will differ with different interest rates.

Income for most retirees is garnered from pensions, profit-sharing plans, Social Security, and do-it-yourself pensions such as individual retirement accounts (IRAs). Federal law requires employers to keep recipients notified with respect to pensions, profit-sharing programs, and any other company-sponsored retirement investments. Read and understand the most recent literature explaining these plans in order to plan effectively.

Types of Retirement Programs

Practically all employer-sponsored retirement plans require the employee to work for a certain number of years to receive certain benefits. This is called *vesting*. Federal pension law does not require employers to offer pensions. It doesn't dictate how much an employer should put into any individual's pension, either. However, the law does require all employers offering pensions to use specific vesting formulas. The vesting formula determines at what time you are entitled to a certain percentage of the money that has been put aside for your pension. Vesting formulas are either *all-at-once* or *phased in*.

The 1986 Tax Reform Act set 1989 as the beginning for new vesting formulas. All-at-once vesting formulas give workers 100 percent vesting after five years of service. The phased-in formula gives an employee 20 percent vesting after three years, then 20 percent per year thereafter. The employee is fully vested after seven years. Employers can choose shorter vesting formulas than that, but not longer ones.

Here is an example of a phased-in formula: During the years of your employment with a company, your employer might have put aside five thousand dollars toward your pension. If you are 60 percent vested, you'd be entitled to 60 percent of the five thousand, or three thousand dollars, at the moment you terminate employment. Those funds might not be payable until a later date. Discuss with your employer the specifics which pertain to your individual case.

Test Your Pension I.Q.

The Employee Retirement Income Security Act of 1974 (ERISA) ensures each employee who participates in a pension plan an adequate retirement income.　　　　　T or F

> *The 1974 law says nothing about the overall size of a pension. A pension may fail to provide an adequate income, even when added to Social Security payments.*

The law guarantees a pension to every American worker.　　　　　T or F

> *The law does not require every employer to offer a pension plan.*

All pensions are insured by the government; you will get exactly what you've been promised.　　　　　T or F

> *Not all pension plans are insured; even a government-insured plan may fail to provide full original benefits in the event an employer cancels the plan.*

After you have worked a specified period of time   T or F
for an employer under a pension plan, ERISA requires that you be given the nonforfeitable right to
certain earned benefits.

> *Yes, this right is called* vesting. *By law, em-*
> *ployer contributions must vest in accordance*
> *with a choice from certain schedules set by the*
> *government. For example, if your employer*
> *chooses a schedule that requires that you be 100*
> *percent vested after five years of service, then*
> *even if you lose your job after five years, you will*
> *eventually be entitled to a pension based on the*
> *pension plan formula.*

Your pension will probably be reduced if you retire   T or F
early.

> *Usually there is a percentage reduction in bene-*
> *fits for each year a person retires before he or she*
> *is 65.*

The law ensures that your spouse will get your full   T or F
pension when you die.

> *Most pension plans are required to provide a*
> *joint-and-survivor annuity provision. If you*
> *and your spouse do not reject the provision in*
> *writing, when you die your spouse is entitled to*
> *receive at least half of your monthly benefits for*
> *life. If you elect these benefits, however, your*
> *monthly pension payment might be lower than*
> *if you had rejected the survivor annuity.*

Employers can fire employees to deprive them of   T or F
their pensions.

*If you think you've been wrongfully denied a
pension, you can take legal action. You will,
however, need to prove there are no valid reasons
for dismissal or for denial of benefits.*

You are entitled to a complete explanation of your　　T or F
pension plan in easily understood language.

*Employers must give each employee a booklet
that clearly describes the pension plan and its
benefits.*

It's your right to know how the money in your　　T or F
pension plan has been and is being invested.

*You have the right to know. If you think your
pension money is being invested unwisely, you
should contact the Administrator of Pension
and Welfare Benefit Programs, U.S. Department of Labor.*

Some pension plans reduce benefits according to　　T or F
your Social Security retirement income.

*Some plans do provide for a Social Security
offset by which your Social Security retirement
benefit is considered when determining your
pension payment. You may be left with little
pension, or none at all.*

Taking Retirement Now or Later?

Should you take early retirement or work as long as you
possibly can?

The answer varies from one individual to another. The
wisdom of taking an early retirement could depend upon the
structure of your pension plan and also upon your work
history. Another one, two, or three years of work could
increase your pension benefits considerably. Determine this

factor as soon as possible, certainly before you make any premature decisions to retire.

Many financial programs offer retirees a choice of taking all of the accumulated money in one lump sum or taking one of a variety of annuity plans. With the lump-sum payment, the money is yours to use as you see fit. You can do a rollover into an IRA rollover account and gain control over the investing of your assets while deferring the payment of taxes. With the annuity plan, you receive a certain monthly payment for a fixed period of time, or for the life of the employee or spouse.

Some employees can choose between annuity programs that terminate when the employed person dies; others pay a smaller amount per month to the ex-worker, and upon his or her death continue payment to a surviving spouse for a certain period of time.

This decision (lump sum or annuity) could be the most important one you will make with respect to your retirement income. Individual situations differ, but here is a typical example.

David Henderson, a retiree, must choose between a $60,000 lump sum payment or a $500-per-month annuity for life. If he chooses the annuity and lives for twenty years, he will have received a total of $120,000 ($500 per month times twelve months equals $6,000 per year, times twenty years equals $120,000). If he lives for thirty years, he will have received $180,000. But if he lives only five years, he will have received only $30,000. If he chooses the lump sum payment, he could invest the entire amount at the current rate of 8 percent per year. This would generate an annual income of only $4,800 or $400 per month (compared to the annuity payment of $6,000, or $500 per month). But that income could continue indefinitely, or until he or his survivors withdrew money from the principal amount.

The trade-off in this case is between a somewhat higher monthly income for a fixed period or a slightly lower income for an indefinite period, plus the availability of the full principal amount (in exchange for the monthly income).

> ### *"Much will depend on . . . being ready, willing, and able to manage your nest egg."*

Which would you choose? The decision can be crucial. Much will depend on the availability of conservative investment opportunities at the time you make the decision, plus your being ready, willing, and able to manage your nest egg, as opposed to having the annuity company manage it for you on a worry-free, carefree basis.

(The foregoing example does not take into account federal income taxes on either the lump sum or the monthly payout plans. Naturally, those would have to be calculated.)

Should you decide to choose the lump sum payout, you might be eligible for favorable tax treatment on that money. If you put otherwise taxable proceeds into an IRA rollover account, you can postpone paying such taxes and earn interest or dividends on the entire sum on a tax-deferred basis until you withdraw the money. The advantage of a rollover account is that you can have control over your investments, because you have more investment choices than you have with an annuity.

It might also be possible to take advantage of a technique known as *averaging*. This allows you to pay the taxes due on the lump sum for the year in which your tax bracket might dictate. Under the 1986 Tax Reform Act, if you were at least age fifty on 1 January 1986, and you receive a lump sum in 1987 or after, you can choose from two different averaging formulas—a five-year plan and a ten-year plan. The advice of a tax counselor is recommended to determine the best choice in your circumstances. Persons under fifty on 1 January 1986 are limited to the five-year averaging plan.

Investing Your Own Pensions

If you earn income from your work, you are eligible for an individual retirement account (IRA). If you are self-employed, you are eligible for a Keogh plan (known as the self-employed person's plan). And if your employer offers the 401(k) plan, you can take advantage of that.

While retired persons should not take excessive risks, they should be aware that leaving their money in simple money markets may be detrimental to their long-term purchasing power. Use the formula in table 4.1 to calculate whether or not your portfolio is maintaining its purchasing power.

Table 4.1 Formula for Calculating Purchasing Power	
Current $ amount	$100,000
plus current earnings	+$6,000
minus taxes	-$1,200 (1)
minus inflation	-$5,000 (2)
equals net value on the portfolio	$99,800
(1) This assumes a 15 percent federal tax bracket	
(2) This assumes a 5 percent inflation rate	

If a negative balance is incurred year after year, the purchasing power of the retirement account could be severely diminished.

THE UNIVERSAL SAFETY NET

A generation ago, the federal government made a law that provides a safety net for people who arrive at the age of

---

"Wouldn't it be nice if you could stop work one month and Uncle Sam would start sending you checks the next month for the rest of your life."

---

retirement without funds to sustain them. The Social Security Administration was part of Franklin Delano Roosevelt's New Deal, arriving with fanfare in 1935 when I was a kid of nineteen. For the first time in history, workers sixty-five and older were guaranteed an income when theirs dried up.

My friend Peter Drucker pointed out in the 16 January 1975 issue of *The Claremont* [College] *Collegian,* that when Social Security began in 1935, seven people received benefits for every one hundred in the labor force.

The Social Security program has changed many times, prompted by the continuing objective of financial soundness for the system while providing comprehensive protection for American families. In 1991, an estimated $265 billion in benefits were paid to approximately 40 million people. Some 133 million Americans are working and paying into Social Security. For additional information write to:

Social Security Administration
Wilkes-Barre Data Operations Center
P.O. Box 20
Wilkes-Barre PA 18711-2030

Income from Social Security Benefits

Wouldn't it be nice if you could stop work one month and Uncle Sam would start sending you checks the next month for the rest of your life, so that you could maintain the standard of living to which you had grown accustomed? Social Security isn't quite that simple. Much planning is necessary to make certain that you receive what you are entitled to.

First, visit the office of the Social Security Administration in your area (call first). Get the most up-to-date literature on benefits that you can find. In addition to retirement benefits, there are provisions for disability benefits, for the survivors of a deceased worker, and for the dependents of a retired or disabled worker. Medicare is also available to those sixty-five and older and to long-term disabled persons; both will be discussed later in this section. The Social Security office can also provide you with an inquiry card, "Request for Statement of Earnings." By completing and submitting that card to the Social Security Administration, you will get a statement of the Social Security earnings that have been credited to your Social Security number. It is wise to check on the accuracy of these amounts. The office can also give you estimates as to the amount of Social Security benefits you'll be entitled to receive upon retirement, but it won't be able to give you more specific amounts until you are at least sixty or within a few months of actual retirement.

In addition to inquiring about your retirement benefits, you should definitely contact your Social Security office if:

- You cannot work because of an injury or illness that is expected to last at least a year.

- You are sixty-two years old and plan to retire soon.

- You are within three months of age sixty-five and can enroll in Medicare, even if you do not plan to retire.

- A worker in your family dies.

- You are age sixty and a surviving spouse.

- You, your spouse, or your dependent child suffers permanent kidney failure.

Social Security benefits are not automatic. You must file
for them on prescribed forms, with specific documentation,
and, for some claims, within certain time limits. Survivor
benefits, in particular, are often left unclaimed because the
survivors do not realize they are available.

Many variables can affect the size of your Social Security
benefits. For example, you may retire as early as sixty-two,
but if you choose to retire before sixty-five, you will receive
a lesser monthly amount than if you wait until age sixty-five.

If you continue working, whether part-time or full-time,
you will lose some or all of your Social Security benefits if
your income from work exceeds a certain annual amount. In
addition, if you continue to work once you have started
receiving Social Security benefits, you will have to continue
paying Social Security taxes on your earnings, as will your
employer. The amount of those taxes will, of course, depend
on your annual earnings. Your benefits also will be recom-
puted to take account of additional earnings so that your
benefits can, in some instances, increase later on.

If your income exceeds a certain amount once you have
started receiving Social Security benefits, a portion of your
benefits will be subject to federal income taxes. Income for
this purpose includes one-half of your Social Security benefits and any tax-exempt interest income. The threshold
amounts are twenty-five thousand dollars for individuals
filing single tax returns, thirty-two thousand dollars for couples filing joint returns, and zero for married individuals
filing separately who lived with their spouses at any time
during the tax year. As much as one-half of your annual
Social Security benefits can be subject to taxation in whatever

tax bracket you happen to fall for that year. If your income from all sources falls below the previously noted amount, you need not worry about this potential tax. But if your income from all sources exceeds those amounts, you will have to do a separate calculation when completing your federal income tax return.

Needless to say, these provisions in the Social Security law strongly influence the feasibility of your continuing to work once you have reached the age at which retirement benefits are available.

Effects of Continued Employment on Social Security Benefits

Many senior citizens find that they must continue working beyond their normal retirement date in order to have the money they need to live comfortably. Others choose to continue working, not so much for financial gain, but for psychological and social benefits. Some happily await the termination of their so-called real job so they can begin a long-desired new career, which may be full time or part time. The reason a person continues working after normal retirement age often determines whether or not such work will require a financial investment on his or her part.

If you continue to work as an employee in the same capacity as before, no financial investment will be required, of course; but don't be surprised if, after you have calculated the net effect of Social Security and other taxes on your income, you find yourself working for less per hour than you may have earned twenty or thirty years ago.

If you intend to make a personal investment to accomplish certain work goals, then you must undertake some very serious planning. Entering the business world—whether starting from scratch, buying an existing business, or investing in a franchise—can be rigorous and challenging. Perhaps the greatest warning to heed is this: embarking on a new business always takes a lot more capital than anticipated. You are risking the depletion of your retirement capital to achieve a hoped-for level of income. And what if that income never materializes? It has long been a rule of thumb that new business ventures do not even break even until between the second and third year of operation. Can you afford to subsidize yourself for that long? Do you want to forego interest or dividends you could have earned by investing your money in a more assured way?

In short, if you have always longed to sell guitars or repair computers or be a chef or make model airplanes, it might make more sense to do that as someone else's employee, at least temporarily, to see if you really do enjoy it. The trial period can save you the potential disaster of losing a large portion of your capital on something that did not work out either financially or psychologically. If, after the trial by ordeal, you still want to proceed with this new career, you can do so with more assurance of success.

In sum, once Social Security checks start coming, you face some hard decisions if you continue to work for a salary. You will have to continue to pay Social Security taxes on your income from work. In addition, if you earn too much from work, you can lose some Social Security benefits and possibly even have to pay some income taxes on those benefits you do receive.

Fill out the following questions to determine whether it will pay you to keep drawing a paycheck.

A. Annual Social Security benefits at age:

      62 $_____
      63 $_____
      64 $_____
      65 $_____

B. How much money can you earn from salaried employment each year before you start losing Social Security benefits? $_____

C. If you earn $_____ (projected earnings) $_____, you will lose $_____ of your Social Security benefits;

D. In addition, you will pay $_____ in Social Security taxes.

E. That leaves you with $_____. Will it pay to work? Are there benefits beyond the financial rewards?

F. If your earnings from all sources (work, investments, etc.) push you into the bracket where your Social Security benefits will be subject to income taxes, how much more will you stand to lose?

INCOME FROM ASSETS

The house they live in is the biggest single source of potential income for most people nearing retirement. Many people in this age group also own their own business or professional practice. The sale of that asset can be a very important source of income. Further, almost everyone owns assets that are not producing income but that could be sold and turned into a source of income.

Equity in a House

If you have owned your house for more than just a few years, you no doubt have acquired tens of thousands of dollars in equity. A combination of inflating values and the reduction of your mortgage debt through the years leaves you with an untapped source of considerable wealth. But how can you turn that wealth into cash in your pocket?

One quick way, of course, is the home equity loan. You've seen the ads: borrow against the equity in your home and have all the cash you want, to do whatever you want .... The only trouble is that you have to pay that money back, and with interest. So, while an equity loan provides a source of income, it also creates debt that has to be paid, and paid on time. And if you borrow merely to create some investment dollars, it is a virtual certainty that you will pay a higher rate of interest on the loan than you will earn on the investment— if it is a safe and prudent investment. To earn more on the investment than you are paying in interest on the loan, you will have to take some risk with the money. If the risk doesn't pan out, you could be a loser all around; you could lose your investment dollars but still have to repay the loan, plus interest.

Like many retirees, you may decide to sell your home and move into more compact quarters. You may choose a smaller house, a condominium, or an apartment. This is an effective way to create more spendable cash and still keep a comfortable roof over your head. However, choosing a different type or different size dwelling is a very personal matter, which we will discuss in another section of this book. If at all possible, you should rent the new quarters for at least a few months before you make the major decision to buy. It is worth the delay to ensure that you will be happy in a different kind of environment.

Selling your home also presents you with another decision: do you want to receive cash for the total amount of the sale, or are you willing to take back the buyer's IOU in lieu of cash? If you do want to cash out, the buyer will have to find financing. If interest rates are high, that could be a problem. At the very least, it could cause some delay in closing the deal. Nevertheless, there is nothing quite as satisfying as walking away from a major transaction with all cash in hand. It eliminates any problems in waiting for monthly payments to come or in being an absentee landlord.

On the other hand, if a buyer is able to make a reasonably good down payment (at least 15–25 percent of the total purchase price), and if the buyer has a good credit history, it might be possible for you to turn your equity into a regular monthly check at an interest rate higher than you could earn through conventional sources.

For example, if you cashed out of the sale of your home and had $100,000 in hand, you could invest it safely in a federally insured savings certificate at a rate of, say, 8 percent. On the other hand, if you took the buyer's IOU, you could expect to earn at least 2-4 percent higher on that same $100,000 debt. This is because home mortgage interest rates tend to run at least 2–4 percent higher than the interest rates payable on certificates of deposit. Naturally, the savings certificate is federally insured, whereas the buyer's IOU is not. But the buyer's IOU is secured by a lien on the house. If he or she fails to pay, you can take the house back and sell it all over again.

There are other ways to turn the equity of your home into income. One way is called the *sale/leaseback*. In this type of arrangement the homeowner sells the property outright to another party, and the buyer simultaneously gives the homeowner a lease on the property, usually with lifetime renewal rights. The seller thus receives a large sum of cash but is required to make monthly rental payments to the new owner. The feasibility of this method depends on the tax benefits available to the parties; it is usually most workable when parents and children are the respective sellers and buyers.

Another method, known as the *reverse annuity mortgage*, involves a lender's making monthly payments to a homeowner. The monthly payments constitute a debt, plus interest, that the owner will have to repay either upon moving out of the house or, via his or her estate, upon the owner's death. This method has been tried by numerous financial institutions in recent years, but to date no one has devised a program that makes it feasible for the broad mass of people.

Before you embark on any program involving a transaction on your home, you should consult an attorney and an accountant for the proper legal and tax advice. There are important income tax implications to selling a home. If you proceed properly, you can save many thousands of dollars in income taxes.

Sale of a Business Asset

Whether full-time or part-time, such interests can represent a greater source of income than you may have suspected. Even the most modest little retail outlet in the most modest location can have some value. The shop may have a steady and loyal clientele, a good lease at advantageous rents, or simply a lot of good will. Any or all of those items can be turned into dollars. Professional practices, even if you have been operating solo, can similarly have substantial value. And most partnerships, if they were properly formed in the first place, will have some form of buy-out arrangement stipulated in the partnership agreement.

Wise selling of an interest in a business or practice will require some legal and accounting advice in advance. You can also obtain counsel from your trade or professional association. The associations also might have means of putting you in touch with interested buyers.

As with selling your home, you will have to decide whether or not you want to cash out of your business or take back the buyer's IOU. The same basic principles prevail in reaching a decision: getting a substantial downpayment, checking the buyer's credit history for reliability, and structuring a good interest rate on the IOU. Structuring the price for the sale of a business or practice can be more tricky than for the sale of a house. It is not uncommon for the sale of a business to be based on a certain fixed amount of money plus a share in the profits that decreases over a period of years.

Again, as with the sale of a house, there would be some concern if the buyer defaulted. If you have cashed out, of course, this problem would not arise. But if your income depends on the continuing success of the business once it is in the hands of the new owner, you should protect yourself to every extent possible.

Your best protection against default is to include a clause in the sale contract that would allow you to hire someone else to run the business for you at the first indication that the buyer is not going to be able to continue making payments. The sooner you can intervene, the better off you will be. Once the business has been run into the ground by a negligent owner, it may be too late to salvage anything. It would also be wise to protect yourself against the unexpected death of the buyer. You can require that a life insurance policy on the buyer be taken out in your name as part of the original sales agreement.

Nonproductive Assets

You may have thousands of dollars worth of personal effects and collected items for which you have no further use. These may include furniture, coins, stamps, precious metals, furs, appliances, tools, works of art, china, silver, crystal, linens, and so forth. Sentimental value is one thing, but cash is something else. By converting any or all of these items into cash and then prudently investing that cash, you can create a source of income that can make the difference between comfort and discomfort in your retirement life. In addition, by selling any of these items upon which you had been paying insurance premiums, you can cancel the insurance and put those premium dollars to more productive use. Seek the counsel of a professional appraiser for any items that you believe to have artistic or antique value. Items that you cannot sell can be donated to your favorite charity or its thrift shop. This will allow you to take a tax deduction (for those who itemize) based on the current market value of the items. Every dollar you save in income taxes is a dollar that you can spend or invest.

INSURANCE ASSETS

Varying levels of income can be obtained through different kinds of insurance plans: health, life, and disability.

> *"You can create a source of income that can make the difference between comfort and discomfort in your retirement life."*

Medicare

Medicare, in effect, provides you with reimbursement to meet some of your hospital and medical costs once you have reached age sixty-five. Medicare is a two-part insurance program operated by the federal government. Part A, the hospital insurance plan, is available to most Americans when they reach age sixty-five, whether or not they are retired. *File for coverage three months before reaching sixty-five.* If you do not enroll in Medicare, you will not be entitled to the benefits. The government does not automatically enroll you. Disabled persons may qualify before age sixty-five.

Part B, the medical insurance plan, is a voluntary program that covers certain doctor's services and other items not covered under Part A. Get further details on Medicare from your Social Security office. Remember that Medicare does not cover all of your healthcare expenses. Large gaps may exist between the Medicare protection and your actual medical expenses. Thus, it is wise, at the earliest possible time, to purchase a supplemental private plan that will fill in *some* of the Medicare gaps. Perhaps such a plan is available as an extension of your group health plan at work.

Life Insurance

Your life insurance needs may be drastically different when you enter retirement than they were in the early stages of your career. Back then you may have had a family to protect; if so, they are likely grown now, and the need to protect them has diminished. Consequently, it may be feasible for you to cut back on the amount of your life insurance. However, first determine whether your spouse or grown children may still need that protection. With ordinary life insurance policies (as opposed to the typical term insurance policy), it is possible to either cash in your policy, borrow a substantial sum of money against it, or convert your insurance to other types of plans. The following table illustrates the conversion values in a typical policy.

Table 4.2 illustrates a policy with a face value of $10,000. At the end of twenty years, as you can see, the cash/loan value is $2,890. That means you can stop paying premiums and cash in the policy for that amount of money. Or you can borrow that amount of money from the insurance company and continue paying premiums on the policy, remaining insured for the original face value less the amount of the loan. In other words, you could have $2,890 in hand and remain

Table 4.2 Life Insurance Conversion Values			
End of Policy Year	Cash or Loan Value	Paid-up Insurance	Extended Term Insurance
5	$590	$1,410	14 yrs. 48 days
10	$1,340	$2,900	20 yrs. 310 days
15	$2,100	$4,130	22 yrs. 288 days
20	$2,890	$5,180	22 yrs. 303 days

insured for $7,110, provided you continue paying the premiums and the interest on the loan. You do not have to repay the loan itself. If the loan is not repaid upon death, then the proceeds payable to the beneficiary will be the lesser amount—the face value minus the loan.

"The premiums that you otherwise would have been sending to the insurance company stay in your pocket and are, therefore, an indirect source of income to you."

Another option is to stop paying premiums and convert the policy to paid-up life (though in some cases you may be better off borrowing the cash value and investing it). In this instance, after twenty years, the amount of paid-up life insurance would be $5,180. Without paying another penny in premiums, you would remain covered for the rest of your life for that amount.

You can also convert to extended term insurance. In this case, you stop paying premiums, and you remain covered for the full face amount of the policy, but for a limited amount of time; at the end of 20 years that time would be 22 years, 303 days. In other words, you continue to be fully insured from the time you stop paying premiums for almost 23 years, at the end of which time the coverage ceases. In all of these instances, of course, the premiums that you otherwise would have been sending to the insurance company stay in your pocket and are, therefore, an indirect source of income to you.

You may have purchased life insurance policies years ago of the endowment type or the paid-up-at-sixty-five type. With those types of policies your values are already at the fullest, and you can start taking an income out of them while still retaining a major portion of the insurance. Check with your agent or the company that issued the policy for specific details on such plans.

Disability Insurance

This protection was beneficial while you were working, but once you stop working, you obviously do not need insurance against being unable to work due to disability. Stop paying premiums for this coverage and keep the money for yourself.

INCOME FROM INVESTMENTS

This broad and very important subject is covered in much greater detail in the investment strategies section. For purposes of this section, we will focus more on the *attitudes* that can lead to a successful income-generating program with your investments.

First, let us define some terms for purposes of this exercise. Let us consider *investing* to mean putting your money to work with a high degree of assurance that it will grow into a known amount of money in a known period of time. And let us consider *speculating* to mean putting your money to work in such a way that you will never know how much money you will have at any future time. The difference, as you can see, is critical. With investing, you know what to expect. With speculating, you don't.

Investing your money so it will provide an assured return covers the arenas of saving certificates (certificates of deposit), government bonds, highly rated corporate bonds, and to a limited extent, some high-quality preferred stocks whose dividends can be relied on and whose market fluctuation is minimal. Speculating, or putting your money to work with no guarantee as to what will happen to it, covers most other arenas: the stock market, real estate, commodities, precious metals, and collectibles.

Many salespersons and institutions—banks, savings and loans, mutual funds, insurance agents, precious metals dealers, municipal bond sellers, and so on—are vying for your money. If someone is trying to sell you something, however, you had best ask yourself if the sale is more in the salesperson's best interests or your own. Not all salespeople of financial products and services have the best interests of their clients at heart. Many of them, it should come as no surprise, have their own best interests at heart. The burden is upon you, the buyer, to beware of all the pitfalls that lurk in financial products, no matter how glowing a pitch the salesperson gives.

Financial institutions are also developing new forms of investment almost as fast as the printing presses can turn out the prospectuses. Many of these new investment techniques are very sophisticated and require a great deal of study. Salespeople will not always tell you everything you need to know, and you may not have the patience to interpret the prospectus, which explains all of the risks and other details. It would be prudent to make up your mind at the outset that you will not invest your money unless you know exactly where it is going, what will happen to it, and how you can get it back, if at all, if you do not like what is happening to it.

Despite all of the new investment vehicles created in recent months and years, there is still nothing that compares with the simplicity, safety, and convenience of federally insured deposits. Naturally, you can get higher returns elsewhere, but you assume a higher risk accordingly. Conservatism is the order of the day. If you make a serious mistake, you might not get a chance to rectify it.

WHAT FINANCIAL INSTITUTIONS OFFER

Once you and your financial advisers have discussed the best way to attain your goals, you'll find a wide variety of financial products and services from which to choose.

Banks, savings and loan associations, and credit unions were originally designed to serve the needs of the business community. They also provided checking and savings accounts, and personal loans for individuals. Savings and loan associations and mutual savings banks, often called thrifts, were established primarily to pool depositors' savings and provide mortgage loans; but now they provide other services as well. Credit unions, which also accept deposits and make loans, are associations of people united by a common bond, often a place of employment. Today there are more similarities than differences among these various institutions.

They all offer generally the following services, although there may be distinctions among individual institutions.

Checking Accounts. In the past, these did not pay interest. Today, many do pay interest if you keep a minimum balance in the account. This type of checking account is sometimes called a NOW account, but different banks have different names for it. Credit unions offer share draft accounts which, for practical purposes, serve as checking accounts for their members. Many of these accounts pay interest. Checking accounts are a great convenience, but you should always find out about minimum balance requirements and service charges before you open an account.

Savings Accounts. These pay interest on your money, although the amount of that interest has traditionally been limited by federal law. With passbook or statement savings you have access to your money whenever you need it, but you may trade some loss of income (when inflation rates are higher than the interest you're earning) in exchange for convenience and security.

Certificates of Deposit or Time Deposits. These have minimum deposit requirements and pay higher rates of interest than is permitted on regular savings accounts. The drawback: you must commit your funds for a set period of time, and you face substantial penalties if you withdraw money before maturity.

Market Rate Accounts. Savings accounts earning fluctuating market rates are called Market Rate Accounts. You may take your money out as you please, but you must maintain a minimum amount in the account at all times in order to earn the higher rate.

Individual Retirement Accounts. The IRA, tax-sheltered account may permit you to put away up to two thousand dollars each year free of taxes. It may be funded through regular savings accounts (which don't earn much interest), through market rate accounts at some institutions, and through certificates of deposit. One word of caution: once you're past age fifty-nine and a half you may withdraw funds from your IRA without any tax penalty. If you're in a fixed-maturity time deposit, however, you may face interest penalties on withdrawal even if you are fifty-nine and a half. Financial institutions are permitted to waive the penalties, but not all do. As you get closer to retirement, therefore, reconsider your IRA funding. You may open a different account as often as you like as long as you don't exceed a total of two thousand dollars in contributions in any one year. You may also transfer your IRA account from one institution to another, without tax penalty.

United States Government Savings Bonds. Readily available at these institutions, as well as through payroll deduction plans, these instruments are worth looking into. EE-bonds now pay a variable rate of interest, tied to an index of treasury bills if they are held at least five years. They are redeemable for cash at any time after the first six months.

Treasury Bills. These fixed-income securities for large amounts are issued by the United States government. They may be bought through commercial banks, usually at a fixed dollar charge. They may also be bought through stockbrokers, also for a fee, or directly through a Federal Reserve Bank.

THE FIVE-YEAR RETIREMENT PLAN

Retirement isn't a single act in time: one day you're working, the next day you're not, while you hope against hope that everything will work out okay. Many people mistakenly view it like that, however. It's a lot wiser financially and psychologically to begin planning your retirement ten or fifteen years in advance. This long-range planning helps to guarantee the lifestyle and financial security you want in retirement.

If the date of your retirement is still ahead, try this five-year retirement plan.

Year 1. Starting roughly two years before actual retirement, review all your previous planning. Project your income during the retirement years using information from the previous sections, especially the section on sources of income. Define your post-retirement needs and your goals and the expenses that go along with them. This section is designed to help you do that.

Year 2. This is the year just before your actual retirement. During this year you should begin to refine and put into effect the spending and investing patterns you have previously outlined for yourself. Take plenty of time. Phase in the new patterns gradually.

Year 3. This is the year in which retirement actually takes place, and the planned income and expense patterns must be adhered to as closely as possible. But by now you'll have had practice under your belt, so the adjustment should be relatively easy.

Year 4. You've been retired for one year now, and you've had a chance to see how well your previously planned income and expense patterns work for you. Don't expect perfection. People change. Circumstances change. During this year, make necessary adjustments to your original plans, within the bounds, of course, of your financial abilities.

Year 5. You've had ample time to experiment, to modify, to learn by trial and error. During this fifth year you should be able to solidify your financial arrangements into a format that will last you indefinitely. Minor tuneups may be needed along the way, of course; and you should be ready, willing, and able to make such changes to your plan. But by this fifth year, you should be comfortable with and in control of your overall financial arrangements.

All of the planning steps—defining income sources, recognizing needs and goals, setting priorities for those needs and goals, and working out budgets—should not be carried out just in your head. They should be written down with your spouse or close friend. The sooner you do this and the sooner you begin testing the actual patterns that you set out for yourself, the more readily you'll adjust to the new circumstances of retirement. This relatively easy exercise will reward you with peace of mind and a sense of self-confidence that may cause your friends to marvel.

CHANGING SPENDING HABITS

Many of your spending habits will change in retirement. When work ceases, two-car families often become one-car families. Wardrobe needs are diminished. Costly lunches in restaurants—common during working days—are replaced by lunches at home or in friends' homes. Leisure pursuits can be done at more convenient times and at lower prices: matinees for movies and shows instead of evening performances; golf on week days instead of weekends; travel during the off seasons, when prices are considerably below those of normal vacation times. It's best to anticipate such changes in your spending habits and incorporate them into your financial plan at the earliest possible time.

COPING WITH INFLATION

Inflation is one of the great dilemmas of our modern age. It cannot be overlooked, nor can it be predicted. During the late 1970s, the Consumer Price Index (which is the accepted measure of inflation) was in double digits year after year. By the mid-1980s, it had fallen to well below 5 percent for several consecutive years. When the inflation rate is high, people are troubled, psychologically as well as financially. When the inflation rate is low, people tend to be too complacent. They don't take defensive measures against the next bout of serious inflation.

Also, there was a unique and brief time during the late 1970s when the rate of inflation exceeded the amount of interest people could earn on their savings plans. In short, by leaving your money in a savings plan, you lost money. Prices were rising faster than people's ability to earn. A sad result of this short-lived phenomenon was that all too many people cashed in their savings plans and, lured by fast-talking salespersons, put their money into risky ventures, often suffering serious losses. Had they left their money in the savings account, it would have not earned as much as they would have liked, but at least it still would have been there.

In the early 1980s Congress changed the regulations that restricted how much interest financial institutions could pay on savings deposits. When institutions were allowed to set their own rates of interest, the typical savings account received a substantial dose of inflation proofing. In other words, savings yields can now increase as inflation increases. This takes a lot of sting out of inflation, especially for people who have well-established savings plans with a variety of maturities that give them the flexibility to take advantage of the best yields as they occur.

MEDICAL AND DENTAL EXPENSES

Approximately 40 percent of health care expenses these days are met by Medicare; 25 percent are covered by employer

---

"Inflation is one of the great dilemmas of our modern age. It cannot be overlooked, nor can it be predicted."

---

health plans, pension plans, supplemental health insurance and Medicaid; the rest (about 35 percent) must be paid by the individual. Apply for Medicare benefits three months before your sixty-fifth birthday. The government will not automatically enroll you. At the earliest possible time, examine the Medicare literature and determine what it does and does not cover. In most instances it will be necessary to obtain supplemental private coverage if you wish to have more of your health care costs covered. (Some employer group health insurance programs will continue into retirement to provide you with Medicare supplemental insurance. Check your personnel office to determine if such applies to you.)

Unlike health insurance, which reimburses you for covered medical expenses charged by any doctor, the health maintenance organization (HMO) might not always allow you to choose your doctor. It will probably, however, reduce your medical expenses enough to offset that inconvenience. If there is an HMO in your area, explore its pricing and service structure.

It's never too early to evaluate supplementary health insurance plans. Most private health insurance policies restrict coverage for pre-existing conditions. If you have a health problem at the time you apply for private health insurance, the policy may exclude paying benefits for treatment of that condition for a fixed amount of time. It's wise to obtain supplemental coverage before any such conditions occur.

In shopping for supplemental health insurance, be certain that you are obtaining the comprehensive protection you need. Many policies will protect you only in the event of hospitalization, and then only for a limited number of dollars per day. Remember that not all medical costs are incurred while in the hospital.

It is also important to consider what arrangements you may need to make to sustain an independent lifestyle should you become disabled or chronically ill. Long-term care insurance is emerging as one way to help cover the potentially devastating costs of extended care. Nursing home expenses run as high as forty thousand dollars per year in some locations. This type of insurance usually pays a fixed amount per day for nursing home stays and/or home health care visits. The amount and duration of the benefits provided vary from policy to policy, and even this type of insurance is often expensive and could have coverage limitations.

COST-CUTTING TIPS

You can help your long range financial planning by implementing a few daily habits such as those mentioned below.

- Take advantage of discount coupons, which are available in newspapers and through the mail. It's not advisable to buy products only because of a discount coupon, but it's plain good sense to take advantage of discounts on products you already use. The pennies saved quickly add up to dollars.

- Pay attention to unit pricing when grocery shopping. Unit pricing, which is available in many stores, shows you the cost per ounce or the cost per pound of most products. Considerable savings can often be realized by buying products in larger containers. (Caution: don't be penny-wise and pound-foolish by buying containers that are too large: the products may spoil before you use them.)

"Nursing home expenses run as high as forty thousand dollars per year in some locations."

- Generic brand products can mean substantial savings, particularly for those items whose quality is relatively indistinguishable from brand name items.

- Pay close attention to special sales and seasonal bargains.

- Buy in bulk whenever possible and practical. If you chip in with friends and neighbors, you might be able to buy many products by the carton or case and realize considerable discounts. Most stores provide such price concessions, but only if you specifically ask for them.

This has been a long chapter. Nothing in it is unimportant. Our Lord had more to say on the subject of money than on heaven. From one vantage point, your money is your very life, for financial resources purchase the things necessary for life.

One for the money is a line from a frivolous child's game, but this chapter about your money is anything but frivolous. Take care in your generosity toward the Lord's work and toward others to lay a proper foundation for yourself and for those you love.

5

VOLUNTARISM: THE LANGUAGE OF LOVE

*This is what I mean when I talk
of "a thousand points of light"—that vast galaxy
of people and institutions working together to solve
problems in their own backyard.*

GEORGE HERBERT WALKER BUSH

*D*uring the worst days of World War II, a wounded G.I. sat up on his cot in a field hospital and watched a volunteer nurse dress the putrid wounds of a wounded soldier. The G.I. shook his head. "I wouldn't do that for a million dollars," he said.

With a smile the nurse replied, "Neither would I."

Voluntarism today is not limited to mobilization for war. It extends to city streets, playgrounds, classrooms, churches, mission fields, camps, and even to such mundane venues as mailing rooms of service agencies. It began a long time ago in Jerusalem when twelve apostles appealed to Jewish Christians in the early church to make certain that Greek widows had enough food to eat and a place to live.

> *"Voluntarism . . . began a long time ago in Jerusalem when twelve apostles appealed to Jewish Christians in the early church to make certain that Greek widows had enough food to eat and a place to live."*

When I was young, voluntarism was rather undramatic service. Volunteers included bell ringers at sidewalk Salvation Army Christmas donation buckets, candy stripers in hospitals, and service club members out doing a variety of activities on behalf of the needy. At my first missionary conference, which I attended in about 1930 as a teen-ager, speakers appealed not for volunteers but for young people to make lifelong commitments to countries far away among unevangelized people. Short-term missionary assignments were unknown.

Things changed with the social revolution of the 1960s. Social researcher Daniel Yankelovich noted that the Baby Boomers (the generation born between 1946 and 1964) "have the ability to look reality in the eye; they won't follow old, outmoded ideas out of sentiment. . . . This generation does not have a sentimental attachment to the old days. If there are new realities, they will face them."[1]

With the falling away of tradition comes a wonderful opportunity for senior citizens. Today people like us in the last third of life are signing on as volunteers in record numbers. We want to see and feel the need and work as partners with those on the scene looking for solutions. If national and international vision is to be extended, short-term service is the key.

With your extra time, how about taking at look at the options for volunteer work open to you? Instead of booking passage on a Caribbean cruise, making reservations for a surfside hotel, or merely staying in the groove of established routine, sign on for a volunteer short-term mission. Call it a vacation with a purpose—a refreshing change for you and your spouse.

The eighties have been called the decade of avarice, but the nineties are shaping up as the age of altruism. From the commander-in-chief on down, the message is clear: get involved.

In a speech before a New York City business group, President George Bush unveiled his plan to promote volunteerism in America and beyond. "From now on in America," said George Bush to the cheering audience, "any definition of a successful life must include serving others." He believes that a democratic system must depend to a high degree on the volunteered time and energy of its members for its maintenance, stability, growth, and development.

A democratic social system—nation, state, community, organization, or group—is reliant on the volunteered time and energy of its members. A democratic social system provides the conditions for a personally satisfying, self-actualizing growth opportunity for each individual.

OPPORTUNITIES ABOUND

Volunteers are not a luxury anymore. If they all stayed home for one day, society in the United States would separate at the seams. Volunteer professionals produce materials in braille, document artifacts in local museums, ladle out soup at urban rescue missions and at mission stations half a world away, file materials and books, minister to the dying, fly planes, assist in blood drives, tend to babies in day care centers, teach skills, answer telephones, and even dress putrid wounds as did many volunteer nurses during the wars of our century.

As this book was readied for the press, a survey by the Independent Sector, an umbrella organization for most of the major charitable groups in the country, reported that 45 percent of those surveyed said they regularly volunteered—and more than a third of them reported spending more time on volunteer work in the last three years. In all, it is estimated that 80 million adults contributed a total of 19.5 billion hours, at a value of about $150 billion.

The United States government in the eighties drastically cut public funding of social services. Many of those cuts affected the youngest and poorest Americans, forcing charitable agencies to pick up where government left off. Volunteer groups today are stepping up their recruiting efforts, reaching out to those they once overlooked—including the elderly and the handicapped.

A governmental agency called RSVP (Retired Senior Volunteer Program) was established by ACTION, the National Volunteer Agency in Washington, D.C., in 1971 to fit volunteer opportunities to the needs of retired people. Half a million retired volunteers are serving through fifty-one thousand local organizations, giving sixty-four million hours of service each year. Retired executives help young people learn building and engineering skills; they tutor refugees in math and English; they play key roles in neighborhood crime prevention programs; they service telephone hotlines; they distribute food, salvage surplus produce from farms, organize libraries in prisons, and serve in whatever way their background skills have prepared them for serving.

In March 1991, the Peace Corps celebrated its thirtieth anniversary. More than 120,000 volunteers have been dispatched to more than 100 developing countries in all parts of the world. Peace Corps programs continue to provide assistance to nations in the traditional areas of development such as agriculture, health, education, community development, environment, and construction. New programs include computer training, small business enterprise, and urban planning. For further information write:

Peace Corps of the United States of America
1990 K St., NW
Washington, DC 20526

Charles A. Larson, a professor of literature at American University, joined the Peace Corps at the age of twenty-four in 1962. "We need the spirit of the Peace Corps," he said in *Newsweek's* "My Turn" forum of the 22 July 1991 issue.

It was a transforming experience. I saw ways of life I would never have seen had I remained within the comfortable domain of my provincial Midwestern upbringing. For the first time, I learned to think of someone besides myself, to consider that there is no single way of observing a problem or answering a troubling question. I discovered that without the mutual tolerance and respect of other peoples' cultures, there is no possibility for harmony in our world.

Retired people, Dr. Larson believes, can lead the way in our do-nothing era.

STEREOTYPES ARE DISAPPEARING

A report in the 10 July 1989 issue of *Newsweek* stated that today's volunteers live in every neighborhood. Increasingly, they are "part of a group organized by employers or religious organizations, which still account for a full 20 percent of volunteer efforts."

Many of the old stereotypes are gone. The upper middle class housewife no longer spends her days at the garden club; today, working women are more likely to be in the trenches, working in humanitarian agencies for the good of the less fortunate. Men, as well, are volunteering nearly as often as women for leadership in agencies like Scouts and Little League.

Some agencies, such as Mothers Against Drunk Drivers (MADD) and AIDS groups, didn't exist a decade ago. Barbara Bush's championship of literacy has drawn much attention to that problem. Self-help groups are one of the fastest growing segments of the non-profit agencies. Organizations exist for everything from adult children of alcoholics to Resolve, for people with infertility problems.

Such social phenomena have caused traditional charities to change direction. Junior Leagues now focus on teenage pregnancy, women's issues, alcohol abuse in the home, and disadvantaged children, to mention a few. More than 50 percent of the Junior Leagues are employed full-time in other jobs.

Could the growing interest in public service of the nineties be a reaction to the excesses of the eighties? The gap is growing between the very rich and the hopelessly poor. Investment bankers are stepping around bag ladies on their way to work.

Once, people made a living; now, they're trying to make their lives and hold body and soul together.

In the late eighties, Stan Curtis, a forty-year-old stockbroker from Louisville, Kentucky, founded Kentucky Harvest, an all-volunteer agency that has distributed 1.6 million pounds of surplus food to the needy. Curtis's organization operates so efficiently that the founder needs no government money. In fact, he has rejected federal grants. "We run it like a business," he says.

Senior citizens, many of them retired, have always given more time than most. Now they are living longer and staying healthier.

Bill Oriol of the National Council on the Aging noted that there is "a genuine feeling that the time has come to make really organized use of older people." His organization has started a very successful program called Family Friends, which pairs older volunteers with children who have serious disabilities. Volunteers assist for several hours a week, providing for the parents a much-needed break. Still other agencies recruit retired people for tutoring or child care.

The idea of public service also attracts young people. Volunteer work is now part of the curriculum in approximately 25 percent of American colleges and of dozens of high schools. California has one of the most extensive efforts. Students in the state's twenty-nine public universities are encouraged—but not required—to perform thirty hours of community service annually. About a quarter of the system's 400,000 students are participating in the program.

Congress continually reviews bills that seek to make community service for young people a national priority. They range from proposals to set up programs like the Civilian Conservation Corps of the 1930s to a plan to give states money to expand volunteer opportunities for youths. One of the most controversial is a recent bill calling for a full-time program of civilian or military service through which volunteers would receive vouchers worth up to twelve thousand dollars per year of service. They could use these vouchers to pay for education, training, or a down payment on a house. After five years the program would replace current student loan programs.

Vacations with Purpose

Growing numbers of retired people are turning their vacations into short-term volunteer missions abroad. They are in mission with Christian friends and fellow church members. They might help a poor congregation in Guatemala, work in a dispensary in Calcutta, or perhaps assist in building a church in Africa. Afterward, for a few days, they might stay on for some deep-sea fishing, hunt for souvenirs, or visit museums, art galleries, and/or farms and ranches.

John Maust reported in the April-June 1991 issue of *Latin America Evangelist* that the number of United States laity taking part in short-term missions projects reportedly grew six times over in the past ten years: from roughly 20,000 to 120,000. In that decade, says Doug Millham who, with his wife, Jackie, organized Discover the World to mobilize Christians for cross-cultural ministry, "the number of groups and organizations doing short-term missions has shot from a few dozen to more than 450.

"Just in the last ten years, short-term mission involvement has probably grown ten-fold in all categories. God is really at work doing something."

Why are so many retired people becoming involved in these short-term missions?

"The motivations are sometimes mixed," observed Dennis Massaro, director of the Office of Christian Outreach at Wheaton College, Illinois. "But what comes out of it ... is real commitment to a lifetime of service and evangelism wherever people find themselves."

John Maust sees early retirees in the ranks of the volunteers, not just baby boomers. In a summary of the traits of the short-term missions phenomenon he wrote:

- Short-term missions is not a phenomenon limited to so-called baby boomers, those born between 1946 and 1964, and affluent singles. Volunteers are also coming from the ranks of early retirees and college and high school students.

- A short-term experience will often lead to an eventual career missionary commitment.

- Increasing numbers of local congregations (not just mission agencies) are sending their own teams.

- After a short-term mission, fired-up participants return home to share their experiences—and often rejuvenate their home churches.

Short-term teams are well received by most fellow Christians in the host countries. Of course, some may charge out to save the world, and in the process create more problems than they solve. But seniors are particularly skilled in moving out as learners and servants to build a true kingdom partnership with other members of the body of Christ. Christians everywhere welcome that. Nationals sense that the newcomers eagerly want to be used by God in new ways. They want

---

"Growing numbers of retired people are turning their vacations into short-term volunteer missions abroad."

---

to be on the cutting edge. Short-term missions provide that opportunity.

Occasionally these short-term opportunities stretch into longer, more effective projects. I think of Denny and Jeanne Grindall, successful florists in Seattle, Washington. They wrestled for some time with the issue of what the Lord wanted them to do in their retirement years. They are warm, committed Christians, and the love of Christ shines through their entire being; but they both admit, "We're just ordinary people . . . very ordinary."

With a map of the world spread out before them, the Grindalls one day pinpointed the country of Kenya, East Africa, and decided to have a look as simple tourists. They put their floral business in the hands of someone they trusted and set out to visit the nomadic Masai people. What they found were tribal people living a primitive life with a poor diet and an extremely low life expectancy rate. The Grindalls saw chickens, pigs, and other animals living with humans in

tiny mud huts. Together, Denny and Jeanne became determined to help improve the lot of these fascinating people.

With determination they returned to Seattle and began
making plans to live for a while among the Masai to see what
they could do to outline programs of community development. First on the list was a program to obtain vitally needed
water, pig pens, and sanitation facilities. They wanted to give
the Masai the benefit of their knowledge of horticulture
which they had learned over many years growing flowers.

In only a few months they were able to see the fruit of
their labors. Unsanitary huts were cleaned out; their diet
improved; children suffering from malnutrition were given
necessary supplements and a better diet. The lives of the
entire tribe living in the hinterlands around the capital, Nai-
robi, were improved through the loving, caring concern of
these Christians who put feet to their prayers.

J. Allan Peterson, founder of Family Concern, knows of
a medical doctor in retirement who struggled with a lack of
self-esteem and purpose. During his career he became outstanding in his medical specialty, receiving much recogni-
tion, honor, and praise. In retirement he was forgotten, unknown by a new generation. "They don't know who I am and
they don't care," he said with despair.

Rather than drop totally out of circulation, he tried
changing his focus. He offered his services part-time at the
downtown mission/homeless shelter of his city and discovered new purpose and meaning to his retirement.

Another friend of Dr. Peterson's was a missionary church
builder. He had been retired from his denomination for
several years and was living in Palm Springs. After living at
a relaxed pace for a few years, he decided that he wanted to
make more of a contribution to the cause of Christ. He
considered three large churches in different parts of the
country, settled on one and offered his services half-time
without remuneration. He sold his place and is moving to
this major church in one of America's large cities, eager to get

going again in the ministry. His fervency was caused by the proper value he placed on the heavenly prize.

An Encouraging Report

As a board member of Focus on the Family, I read carefully reports of volunteers published in the organization's publication and in chapel meetings at headquarters. In the September 1990 edition of *Focus on the Family,* author Doris Fell told of her encounter with Sabrina, a volunteer firefighter whom she met in a quaint restaurant and hotel beneath the craggy mountains in Index, Washington.

> I was intrigued by her light brunette hair twirled in a singular, waist-length braid. Between customers, the attractive 26-year-old waitress told me she's been a volunteer on the town's fire department for four years. Three of the nine volunteers are women.
>
> "Last Sunday I was rock-climbing the mountain wall," she said as she poured coffee. "That's when the fire alarm sounded."
>
> I tried to visualize Sabrina rappelling down the wall, grabbing her bicycle and pedaling pell-mell to the firehouse. But it was even more difficult to imagine her decked out in yellow bunker gear and a red fire helmet. And I never could picture her grabbing a fire hose or climbing a ladder and cutting holes in the roof with a chain saw.
>
> On my way out of town, I stopped by the well-kept, framed firehouse where two pumpers and a tanker were parked. I spoke with one of the volunteers, a wiry, bearded young man with dark hair and a pleasant smile. "Volunteer firefighters," he stated, "are the largest group of volunteers in the world."
>
> I couldn't prove his statement, but I sensed his pride. "We're a small town—a small community. We all need to volunteer for something. That's why I'm a fireman."

Doris Fell also told of Helen, an outgoing Christian widow in her early sixties, who keeps busy directing women's retreats, social activities for her church, and Bible study groups in and around her city. Helen learned about the Court-Appointed Special Advocate (CASA) program that works on behalf of abused and neglected children. Volunteers with this agency act as the child's advocate during the long court process.

That suited Helen well. She saw it as "a chance to witness . . . because I was free to pray and love these families." She's creative in dealing with her little charges—a romp in the park, stopping downtown for a sandwich—as she monitors visits with siblings and parents, reviews the social files, checks on school attendance, medical records, and judicial procedures.

A big part is meeting with parents of the children. Says Helen, "Although they know I may have to advocate against them, they see me as a friend—an independent person hearing their side."

Helen often recommends parenting classes to help them become adequate parents—not perfect, but adequate. Helen's court reports and recommendations, made with the best interests of the child in mind, often help the judge determine the child's permanent placement, whether back in the home or with a foster or adoptive family.

Other volunteers in Doris's article include Mildred, eighty-nine, a tall great-grandmother who daily prays for missionaries; Barbara, the founding president of a local adult day care center where Doris's mother was helped so extensively, who "leaned in close" to her elderly charges and became personally involved; Dorothy, a registered nurse retired from service in Zaire, who keeps up an extensive correspondence worldwide with workers like herself who gave their lives in selfless service; Pat, who in her retirement reads to seniors at centers in various parts of her city; Jessie, who is on call to minister in homes of alcoholics; Libby, who is the senior adult coordinator and director of an Alzheimer Support Group sponsored by her church.

Send Me, Lord

Russ Undlin, sixty-five, spent most of his career in international sales. He committed his life to Christ in his middle teens with no grandiose salvation experience, but remained a nominal Christian until recommitting his life in his mid-forties.

Having owned his own business for more than twenty years, he began to experience uncomfortable pressures. Life became a challenge just to stay alive, to meet the pressures of inflation and competition. The work had become repetitive, a quality which he could not tolerate. He made a decision: it was time to retire.

Not wanting inactivity, he answered a Food for the Hungry ad about voluntarism through the International Hunger Corps. Russ and his wife, Betty, drove to Scottsdale, Arizona, to investigate and later signed up. After extensive training they set out for Mozambique.

Russ was troubled by what he saw there. Starvation was not the problem so much as the people's functional disability. While traveling on business trips, he had always merely stepped over the helpless, suffering bodies, thinking, *They could make it if they got up earlier and worked a little harder.* But after experiences in Mozambique he realized that the world's helpless are just that—truly helpless. On a human level, in the real world, they are not going to make it, period. They will falter and die. Thanks to his volunteer experience, Russ now looks at the world's helpless, and especially the American homeless, with different eyes.

"There is a wealth of untapped talent in the retired community that must be put to use," said Russ. "The most ordinary retiree has much to offer that a developing country needs—even the most elementary knowledge that makes a society function."

He cites the example of Mozambicans who discarded their hand scythes because they became dull. No one knew the scythes could be sharpened. "Any one of us can teach his struggling brother how to sharpen a blade, take a bath, boil polluted water, or give a baby who is dying of diarrhea replacement fluids," he said.

The most positive part of Russ's experience was "seeing futility and being able to give part of myself to relieve it, seeing people respond to my offerings and improve their lot in life. The difficult part seemed to be the age gap between myself and other workers. My years of organizing and managing were often in conflict with my younger peers. Diplomacy and special care were necessary to make it work."

At the age of sixty-four, Shig Saimo is retired and living with his wife, Doreen, in Sedona, Arizona, after enjoying his career as a landscaper. For years, he and his wife searched for God through various philosophies and religions such as Buddhism, Hinduism, New Age, and metaphysics. Not until 1975, when Shig and Doreen attended a Johnny Cash movie, did they discover Christ. Doreen responded to the altar call immediately following the movie, but Shig hesitated for another week. Finally he thought, *What do I have to lose?* That day he received Jesus as his Lord and Savior.

After seeing a Food for the Hungry magazine advertisement, Shig wrote for literature. The need for people with backgrounds in agriculture and community development work prompted Shig to sign up. Since he was interested in furthering the Gospel as well, the fit appeared perfect.

Shig has peace about his decision. Rather than taking life easy in a cabin in the country as he had planned, he now has a new course, a new commitment, a new beginning. He wants to go to the "uttermost parts where there is extreme poverty, where there is no electricity, flush toilets or running water like we're accustomed to." Considering the personal inconvenience, Shig says, "I realize the hardships, but they need the gospel and that's where we need to be—where other people don't want to be."

Unbridled enthusiasm flowed naturally from sixty-eight-year-old Roger Hamilton as he told his story of volunteerism. After retiring in June 1988 from his twenty-year career as a community college teacher, Roger and his wife, Grace, started the active retirement both had planned for.

> *"People should not retire from something, but retire to something" (Margaret Collins).*

As volunteers at a missions agency in California, Roger and Grace were introduced to work around the world. Serving in Japan especially interested both Roger and Grace, so they sought God's will and signed up. Roger believes that "every Christian is either a sender or a sent one. We wanted to be sent."

Margaret Collins is a gentle, caring sixty-two-year-old lady with a beautiful southern accent. Most recently, she was the director of child nutrition programs of the Lincoln County Schools in North Carolina. She investigated the possibilities of foreign service through the Peace Corps but settled instead upon an evangelical Christian agency. Margaret is on her way to Addis Ababa, Ethiopia, where political turmoil and war rule the environment. "I have a lot of anxiety trying to get everything done in closing up my mother's home," she says, "but I feel mostly peace. I feel that people should not retire from something, but retire to something. There are so many wonderful things in this world to see and to do and to be part of. I feel sorry for those who just sit and wait for death to come."

Stretch your limits. Find a stretching partner to encourage you in your quest. Chart your progress as you pray and work toward a goal. The greatest tragedy in the world is not physical neglect. It's having no one to say, "You're important." That may be the greatest gift retired people can give to others through voluntarism, the language of love.

6

TAKE CHARGE OF YOUR HEALTH

Health and cheerfulness mutually beget each other.

ADDISON

Nothing is more disconcerting than entering into senior years with health problems. Not all are caused by heredity, accident, or a poor environment in the workplace. Some are avoidable by carefully paying attention to basic rules of good health. If you have health, you have wealth.

LIFESTYLE MATTERS

Today's seasoned citizens are better educated, healthier, and more active than any in history. Old is no longer a synonym for sick, dependent, and problems. If you report a complaint and your doctor tells you you're just getting old, don't buy it. Modern medicine understands the aging process better than ever. Thanks to improved nutrition, better personal health habits, improved medical diagnosis, and better health care, older Americans are entering retirement stronger than ever.

And retirement years aren't necessarily a time to slow down and do less. It isn't true that physical decline is an inevitable consequence of aging. Some people at seventy are more spry and athletic than people thirty-five or forty. The President's Council on Physical Fitness and Sports reported that much of the physical frailty attributed to aging is actually the result of muscular disuse and poor diet. Many such problems, the council found, can be halted, or even reversed, through proper eating habits and a regular exercise program. Good exercise and proper eating habits can stimulate the formation of new bone tissue, and improve cardiovascular endurance, muscle strength and flexibility.

In the United States, fewer than half of all people of retirement age engage in regular, vigorous exercise. Unfortunately, most of them also believe that they get all the exercise they need. One reason may be that many persons are unfamiliar with what constitutes good exercise. Activities often associated with exercise and sports do not attain adequate levels of exertion to generate the desired physical changes in our bodies.

Regular exercise can change a retired person's level of fitness to that of a person ten to twenty years younger. No matter at what age you begin, or for how long you may have been inactive, proper exercise will always improve your physical condition.

Don't expect overnight results, but if you stick with it, you will see progress. Anyone who tries to exercise beyond his or her level of ability or endurance is inviting discomfort or injury. Before beginning, have a thorough physical examination. Discuss your program with the physician and follow the doctor's advice.

FINDING HELP

Alex Comfort, one of the world's leading gerontologists, estimates that more than half of the diseases of the elderly are sociogenic, foisted upon them by society. Old age, he writes, is a trip that society lays on the old, telling them that at a given point—sixty-five, widowhood, or some other arbitrary point—they are henceforth to become drab, spiritless, useless, incompetent, and on and on, even though the day before they may have held the highest power and esteem among their peers.[1]

"Some people at seventy are more spry and athletic than people thirty-five or forty."

Most people of retirement age have at least one health problem. The most frequent are arthritis (46 percent), hypertension (38 percent), hearing impairments and heart conditions (28 percent each), sinusitis (18 percent), visual and orthopedic problems (14 percent each), arteriosclerosis (10 percent), and diabetes (8 percent).

Let's spend a few paragraphs looking at the causes, early warning signs, and professionally accepted treatments of the most common medical problems seasoned citizens face. I know whereof I speak. A jeep accident during World War II when I was in the Army left me with an injury that gave me a limp but didn't impair my moving about or the enjoyment of playing golf.

Diseases

Many of the most difficult medical problems older people face are caused by diseases. Modern medical advances have taken away much of the hopelessness formerly associated with these diseases. Let's examine a few of the most common ones.

Arthritis. This major crippler can make ordinary tasks painful and/or impossible. It is one of the oldest diseases in medical history, currently affecting more than thirty-one million Americans.

Don't buy into the so-called miracle cures—pills, potions, bracelets, and other promises of relief. In ferreting out postal frauds, the United States Postal Service warns that any promise that seems too good to be true usually is. Investigate completely any advertisement before buying it, but especially when it comes to your health.

A sufferer can improve life greatly by developing a positive mental attitude. If a crochet or knitting needle becomes unwieldy, try knitting with larger patterns and thicker yarn, for example. If you can no longer sew, teach a grandchild how to follow in your footsteps.

The National Institute of Arthritis and the Arthritis Foundation cancels out diet as having anything to do with either causing or curing arthritis. Such diets abound, but they can offer no proven relief. Watching your weight can help by putting less strain on joints. People with gout ought to avoid overindulgence in liver, sweetbreads, and kidneys because these foods aggravate their condition.

The United States Food and Drug Administration advocates the use of plain aspirin and asks consumers to avoid more expensive aspirin labeled "arthritis strength," or "arthritis pain reliever." Buy the cheapest aspirin available.

For more information write:

Arthritis Foundation
Room 1101
3400 Peachtree Road, NE
Atlanta, GA 30326

National Institute of Arthritis, Diabetes, and Digestive and Kidney Diseases
National Institute of Health, Building 31, Room 9A04
Bethesda, MD 20892

Cancer. The very word strikes fear in the hearts of most people. Older people succumb the most quickly to cancer. It occurs mostly in people over fifty. Three out of ten Americans may develop cancer, but medical science has made enormous strides in treating many types and in helping to prevent others. Both heredity and lifestyle (smoking cigarettes, drinking alcohol, and eating certain types of food) play a part. Women should have regular checkups to detect lumps in the breast. If you have no doctor or nurse to teach you how, call the Cancer Information Service at 1-800-4-CANCER.

Memorize these warning signs:

- *Lung Cancer*: A cough that won't go away; coughing up blood; shortness of breath.

- *Breast Cancer*: A lump in the breast, change in breast shape; discharge from the nipple.

- *Colon and Rectal Cancer:* Difficulty or pain while urinating; the need to urinate often.

- *Uterine, Ovarian, or Cervix Cancer in Women:* Bleeding after menopause; unusual vaginal discharge; enlargement of the abdomen; pain during intercourse.

- *Skin Cancer:* Sore that does not heal; change in shape, size, or color of a wart or mole; sudden appearance of a mole.

Report to your doctor immediately any of these symptoms. Ask questions. Write down your doctor's answers.

Write for the free government pamphlet "Cancer Prevention: Good News, Better News, Best News." It gives advice on what you can do to protect yourself against cancer. A second free pamphlet, "Everything Doesn't Cause Cancer," discusses the causes and prevention of cancer. Write:

S. James Consumer Information Center
P.O. Box 100
Pueblo, CO 81002

When ordering two or more free pamphlets, please add one dollar to help defray mailing costs.

Diabetes. This disease develops when the body cannot properly convert food into the energy needed for daily activity. When the nondiabetic person eats starches and sugars, the body converts them into a specific sugar called glucose. This in turn combines with insulin produced in the pancreas to enter the cells and later be used for energy. Insulin is not produced or is unavailable in the diabetic's system.

This is a self-help disease. Stick to a diet, keep your weight down, get plenty of exercise, and take prescribed medication in order to enjoy a happy and productive life. More information is available from:

The American Diabetes Association
Box AP
2 Park Avenue
New York, NY 10016

A free publication titled *Dealing with Diabetes* is available from:

Age Pages
National Institute on Aging
Building 31, Room 5C35
Bethesda, MD 20892

High Blood Pressure / Stroke. An estimated sixty million Americans suffer from hypertension (high blood pressure). It can't be cured, but it can be controlled by diet and medication.

Take advantage of free senior citizens testing centers in your area. Lower your intake of salt. Keep off excess fat. New research shows that potassium—found in bananas, potatoes, orange juice, raisins, and melons—can help reduce your risk of hypertension. One study found that women who were given calcium supplements to prevent osteoporosis saw their blood pressure go down to rates closer to normal.

If your doctor has prescribed an antihypertensive drug, it probably means that you will need to take it for the rest of your life. Even if you feel better, don't stop taking it. Once embarked on the road to a low-cholesterol, low-salt diet, don't turn back.

Hypertension can cause kidney failure and stroke as well as heart disease. A stroke occurs when a blocked artery starves the brain of blood. In other cases, a ruptured artery spills blood directly into the brain or its surrounding areas. Both types can cripple or kill. Prevention, again, is the best treatment for stroke. For more information write:

High Blood Pressure Information Center
120/80 National Institutes of Health
Bethesda, MD 20892

Two excellent pamphlets are "Understanding Stroke" and "Handy, Helpful Hints for Independent Living After Stroke." Write for other information on the subject to:

National Easter Seal Society
2023 West Ogden Avenue
Chicago, IL 60612

Influenza. The common flu bug, easily handled by young people, is often life-threatening to the older person. Lowered resistance can allow flu to cause complications for older adults: pneumonia, infected lungs, sore nose and throat, to name only a few.

Learn to detect pneumonia symptoms early (chills, coughing, high fever, chest pain) and get medical help immediately.

The thermostat of an older person is different from a youngster's. When Aunt Esther came calling, she could sit comfortably in the summer heat and might ask us to turn up the thermostat. The most susceptible are the chronically ill, the poor who can't afford enough heating fuel, and older people who forget to take steps to keep warm. Older people don't shiver, and so they don't produce the same body heat as younger people when they need it. Strange as it might seem, older types who have felt cold for years may actually have a lower risk of accidental hypothermia.

In cold weather, set the room temperature at sixty-five degrees Fahrenheit or higher. Dress warmly even when indoors, eat enough food, and stay as active as possible.

In hot weather, stay indoors out of summer heat. Replace water loss by drinking large amounts of cool water or other beverages. Avoid heavily iced drinks. Salt tablets are usually unnecessary and might be dangerous.

For more information, write:

"A Winter Hazard for the Old: Accidental Hypothermia"
National Institute on Aging/Hypo
Building 31, Room 5C35
Bethesda, MD 20892

"Don't Be Beat By the Heat" Poster (D12200)
American Association of Retired Persons
1909 K Street, NW
Washington, DC 20049

National Campaign on Heat and Cold Stress
The Center for Environmental Physiology
Suite 1100
1511 K Street, NW
Washington, DC 20005

Osteoporosis. Back in East Cleveland, Ohio, where I grew up, my parents would take us on frequent visits to my Aunt Esther's house. She had a widow's hump, or osteoporosis. Mother would tell my sister, "Now stand up straight and drink your milk. You don't want to grow up to be stooped over like Aunt Esther."

This disease, often called dowager's hump or brittle bone disease, afflicts more than fifteen million Americans. It strikes one in four women over the age of sixty and can be both painful and crippling. It is eight times more common in women than in men because the bones of females are less dense than males and because pregnant and breast-feeding women often lose calcium from their bones to supply the needs of their developing babies. Women live longer than men, thereby putting themselves at greater risk.

If you are a woman between the ages of forty and fifty-five, maintain a high calcium intake and take extra vitamin D. Consult a gynecologist concerning your need for estrogen.

Natural Effects of Aging

It is a fact of life that our senses lose their sharpness as we age. Although we may not be able to avoid these natural effects of aging, we can make use of the many medical resources available. These resources can help extend physical independence and social involvement to levels unprecedented in earlier decades.

Balance. Organs of sense tell you when you're right side up and how you are moving along through space. These organs, with age, grow less sensitive as instruments. Sudden movements might cause a person to stagger. Add poor sight to such a situation and the danger is compounded.

An easy solution is to move more slowly. Take plenty of time for your walk. Even if you are not lame, take a cane along. If you are shopping in London, ask for a walking stick; if you ask for a cane, you will be given the directions to a store selling teachers' supplies.

A light cane can be a pleasant aide. You'll feel safer and avoid accidents if you wear shoes with rough soles. Fasten miniature crampons to the soles when you walk on icy surfaces.

With a bit of care, you'll feel better about getting around and you'll do it more often.

Care of the Feet. Corns, calluses, warts, and fungal or bacterial conditions such as athlete's foot, dry skin, bunions, and ingrown toenails visit us. Here are some tips to avoid this suffering:

Apply body lotion with either petrolatum or lanolin to legs and feet daily. Use mild soaps, especially those containing cold cream. Avoid prolonged friction from shoes. Trim toenails regularly. Diabetics especially are prone to sores and infections on their feet. Avoid extremely cold or hot baths water, keep the feet dry, and avoid stepping on sharp objects or dirty surfaces.

Constipation. Senior citizens are five times more likely than younger people to have problems with constipation. The problem is probably overemphasized, but remember, a person is only as healthy as his colon.

Avoid filling your stomach with laxatives on a regular basis. Instead, eat more high-fiber foods such as whole grains, vegetables, and fruits. Avoid too many meats, dairy products, eggs, and rich desserts. Drink plenty of liquid as well.

Hearing Impairment. A violin concert, the chimes of a grandfather's clock, the song of the first robin in springtime, a grandchild's warm greeting on the telephone, the television on a long, lonely night—these sounds can lift older people out of isolation and loneliness. Many people of retirement age miss these sounds, or strain to hear them. What beauty and enjoyment they miss.

Practically everybody in the United States begins to suffer some hearing loss by the age of thirty. The rate of loss doubles and triples with each succeeding decade. More people have hearing disorders than heart disease, cancer, blindness, kidney disease, tuberculosis, and multiple sclerosis combined.

- 15 percent of those 55–64 years of age

- 24 percent of those 65–74 years of age

- 39 percent of those 75 years of age and older

For some fifteen million Americans, the loss is severe enough to interfere with their ability to function in a world of sound and speech. Another two million Americans are totally deaf. What causes hearing loss? Facts other than simple aging may contribute, including noise, injury, medication, disease, and heredity. Antibiotics such as streptomycin and erythromycin, diuretics, and large dosages of aspirin

---

"It is a fact of life that our senses lose their sharpness as we age. Although we may not be able to avoid these natural effects of aging, we can make use of the many medical resources available."

---

can be ototoxic—a term used to describe medications that can damage the structures of the inner ear. Heart or kidney disease, diabetes, emphysema, or stroke may disrupt the blood flow to the inner ear, causing permanent hearing loss.

If you know someone with a hearing problem, take these steps to improve communication.

- Speak slightly louder than normal, but don't shout or speak too rapidly. Don't over articulate. This distorts the sounds of speech and makes use of visual clues more difficult.

- Speak to a person at a distance of only three to six feet. Position yourself near good lighting so that your lip movements, facial expressions, and gestures can be clearly seen.

- Don't speak directly into someone's ear. You can't give any visual clues that way.

- If your words are not understood, rephrase the idea in short, simple sentences.

- Treat the hearing-impaired person with respect in order to alleviate feelings of isolation.

Hearing aids have been much more slowly accepted than eyeglasses, possibly because those who first wore them were usually particularly hard of hearing and hence were often avoided by others. Manufacturers consequently tend to emphasize concealment.

A small earphone can be plugged into the phonograph, radio, or television set for your individual use. That will keep neighbors from complaining. Beware of the temptation to enjoy too much of the once familiar level of sound produced by headphones; it can do further damage to your ears. Earphones can keep you from hearing the telephone, doorbell, or dog barking and racing about when the phone rings or the doorbell sounds.

B. F. Skinner, professor emeritus of Harvard University, was once invited home for dinner in Evanston, Illinois, by a professor at Northwestern University. He was seated in a rather dark corner beside the wife of the chairman of the psychology department. The woman, who happened to be Chinese, pointed to what looked to Dr. Skinner as a thick, dark patty; but he did not hear what she said about it. Having admired Chinese cooking before, he attacked the patty with knife and fork. It had the kind of crispy crust he had admired before in Chinese cooking. After he ate it, he noticed the young woman beside him peeling hers. He had eaten a hard-boiled egg, shell and all.

For more information about hearing loss write for a free brochure:

"Facts About Hearing Aids"
Better Business Bureau
1515 Wilson Blvd.
Arlington, VA 22209

The free Age Page fact sheet, "Hearing and the Elderly," discusses all aspects of hearing loss and treatment. Write:

National Institute on Aging
Building 31, Room 5C35
Bethesda, MD 20892
American Academy of Otolaryngology—
Head and Neck Surgery, Inc.
1100 Vermont Ave., N.W., Suite 302
Washington, DC 20005
American Speech-Language-Hearing Association
10801 Rockville Pike
Rockville, MD 20852
National Hearing Aid Society
20361 Middlebelt Road
Livonia, MI 48152

You can learn more about hearing impairment by calling or writing for additional information.

The Alexander Graham Bell Association for the Deaf
2417 Volta Place, N.W.
Washington, DC 20007
(202) 337-5220

Taste and Smell. Foods in your senior years will not taste as good as they once did. You may be inclined to eat less of such food. Less saliva will flow and so you may have trouble swallowing.

To overcome the difficulty here, season your food a bit more and sip a drink as you eat. A dry mouth can mean trouble for your teeth, about which your dentist will advise you. If your voice is scratchy because of dry throat, try sugar-free mints or throat lozenges.

The loss of smell can be a blessing in this increasingly polluted world, but it can be a danger, too. You might fail to smell dangerous fumes or smoke. Be sure to install a smoke detector and be doubly careful about keeping clean and about odors in your own clothing and living area. These affect relationships with other people.

Touch. Fingertips of seniors become less sensitive. You reach out to pick up a cup, misjudge the firmness of your grasp, and drop it. Heavier plates, glasses and cups, and knives and forks, will be easier to handle. To keep from missing pages of thin paper, note the page numbers routinely. And you have good reason also to note the serial numbers when you separate bills fresh from the mint.

Urinary Incontinence. One person in ten over the age of sixty-five has a problem with loss of urine control, or urinary incontinence. The problem is especially common in older women, but it occurs also in men. Aunt Harriet might decline invitations to church; Uncle George might find an excuse for not joining his friends for a round of golf—all because of the fear of not being able to keep a full bladder from leaking.

Seek medical attention to determine the cause of incontinence. Some cases can be cured. For more invitation write:

Help for Incontinent People
P.O. Box 544
Union, SC 29379

Vision. More than half the people over sixty-five have some noticeable loss in vision. Properly fitted eyeglasses are, of course, essential. They should stay in place without fussing with them. While reading, make sure you are not holding your head at an uncomfortable angle in order to get a good light.

A large lens mounted on a floor stand will enlarge type and can be surrounded by a helpful fluorescent ring. A large hand lens is handy for reading small print. With a pocket or purse flashlight, you will be able to read menus in dark restaurants and get about in dark places. Books with large type are available from your public library. The Reader's Digest (Pleasantville, New York 10570) issues a large-print edition available to anyone. Most publishers of the Holy Bible offer large-print editions.

If your peripheral vision has grown weak, learn to look in new ways. In crossing streets, look farther to the right and left than you once did and look both ways to avoid being run down by a cyclist (or jogger) who is going the wrong way. Watch other people and use them as guides. If you cannot easily judge depth, learn to watch how curbs and steps change as you approach them; you can thus get a better idea of how high they are before you step down. If you have lost part of your field of vision, as in glaucoma, remember the deceptive effect of the blind spot. You are not really seeing all of what you are looking at even though you are not aware of gaps in it. When searching for something that you have dropped or lost, cover the area carefully and systematically.

It also helps to simplify your world, as blind people necessarily do. If your vision is really poor, get rid of things you don't need—in particular, things that cause trouble because you can't see them easily. Clean out your cupboards and bookshelves. Small, bright-red, pressure-sensitive markers can be put on things that are especially hard to find or often needed. Whenever possible, avoid the unhappy consequences of not seeing things clearly.

Dry eyes need specially prescribed eyedrop solutions. Excessive tears might be a sign of increased sensitivity to light, wind, or temperature changes. Sunglasses might help. Tearing might be the symptom of a serious eye problem including infection or a blocked tear duct. For detailed information, write:

National Eye Care Project
P.O. Box 7424
San Francisco, CA 94120

> *"Health quackery is a
> ten-billion-dollar business in the
> United States each year."*

HEALTH FRAUD

Don't laugh at people who empty their savings in order to travel outside the borders of the United States for treatment for cancer offered by maverick doctors; don't scoff at the idea of wearing a copper bracelet to cure arthritis, or spending three hundred dollars for a miracle spike to cure cancer; don't be surprised when you learn that someone has spent their last dollar for moon dust through a mail-order Congo Kit.

Health quackery is a ten-billion-dollar business in the United States each year, according to the Health Subcommittee of the House Select Committee on Aging. Unfortunately, too many of the victims are older types like those of us in retirement. Medical fraud extorts not only its victims' money, but their health as well. Add to that the emotional trauma of disillusionment, pain, and delayed treatment and the cost is staggering.

Always be skeptical of unproven remedies whose common elements are conscious deceit, profit, and disregard for scientific fact. None of the products fulfill their claims; some are dangerous. Even those that are not life-threatening can cause a patient to delay seeking necessary medical attention, thereby minimizing your real chances of finding a cure. For more a number of free brochures write to:

Food and Drug Administration
Office of Consumer Affairs, HFE-88
5600 Fishers Lane
Rockville, MD 20857

"Tips on Medical Quackery"
Council of Better Business Bureaus
1515 Wilson Blvd.
Arlington, VA 22209[2]

TEN MYTHS ABOUT AGING[3]

1.	Most older people are sick and senile.	False
2.	Most older people are dependent on their families.	False
3.	People become ever more alike as they get older.	False
4.	After the age of sixty-five, mental abilities begin to fail.	False
5.	Older people have a hard time learning anything new.	False
6.	People should retire at sixty-five because they become less productive.	False
7.	Older people have no interest in sex.	False
8.	Older people are stubborn, "cranky," and set in their ways.	False
9.	Older people are isolated and lonely.	False
10.	Most old people live in nursing homes.	False

LEGAL AND ESTATE PLANNING

*Whatever failures I have known,
whatever errors I have committed, whatever
follies I have witnessed in private and public life have
been the consequences of action without thought.*

BERNARD BARUCH

You've seen the motto "Plan Ahead" on a friend's desk or on the wall of an office. The last few letters are crowded into the space, proving that the creator of the motto failed to take his own advice. That describes a lot of people who look to their senior years without having planned ahead properly to assure them of needed resources.

ASPECTS OF ESTATE PLANNING

Perhaps no area requires sound advice more than that of estate planning, which is a subject of paramount importance in a person's middle years. Your estate is the sum total of all that you own, plus all that is owed to you, minus all that you owe. Upon your death, your estate becomes a legal entity in its own right: the estate of John or Jane Doe. The estate then consists of all the assets and debts you had while alive.

Estate planning helps you to plan for the use or distribution of your assets according to your needs and desires. Putting your financial and other assets in order is a good idea, no matter what the size of your estate.

Careful estate planning should enable you to do the following:

- Make arrangements that will minimize state and federal taxes on your estate.

- Arrange your affairs to minimize the probate and administrative costs connected with your estate.

- Assure distribution of your estate so your spouse, children, and other heirs may be provided for as you wish.

- Consider how readily your assets can be converted into cash. This could be important to your heirs if they are confronted with unexpected expenses in settling your estate.

- Assure that your estate will be settled with a minimum of red tape.

Most important, careful estate planning provides you with peace of mind about the welfare of your family after your death.

There are two essential elements in estate planning: (1) arranging your assets so that they can be distributed with maximum ease and minimum cost, and (2) setting forth binding instructions so that your assets are distributed and your other wishes are carried out as you desire. Step one involves understanding your present and future financial status and making modifications as needed. Step two requires defining just what it is you want to accomplish.

Spread out before me just now are booklets, magazines, official reports, computer printouts, and brochures from official sources and from my friends. They all say essentially the same thing: start early, get expert advice, and make

---

"Careful estate planning provides you with peace of mind about the welfare of your family after your death."

---

necessary changes as you go along to keep your estate in apple pie order. Of specific help have been the American Association of Retired Persons, the Special Committee on Aging of the United States Senate, the United States Department of Health and Human Services, and the Pension Benefit Guaranty Corporation in Washington, D.C.

Steps in Estate Planning

1. Gather information on your current income and expenses.
2. Develop a budget for today.
3. Develop a statement of net worth.
4. Estimate your retirement income and expenses.
5. Plan your retirement budget.

Your Estate Planning Team

Estate planning requires time and study. Don't expect it to be easy or quick. While you may feel competent to do this work yourself, you would be wise to seek professional advice. A team approach to estate planning is usually best. The members of the team might be a lawyer, an expert accountant, a banker, and an insurance agent.

The lawyer is probably the most important person on your team. He or she can help you to determine which of several devices—will, trusts, gifts, and so forth—would be best for protecting and eventually passing along wealth to your survivors. The lawyer can also prepare the relevant documents and see that they are properly signed and witnessed.

The task of selecting a lawyer is a lot like choosing a doctor. You will want someone in whom you can confide, who will sympathize with your problems, and who will respect your pocketbook. In many situations you may need a lawyer who specializes in a particular field. Here are some suggestions for choosing your lawyer.

- Ask friends about their experiences with specific lawyers.

- Ask other professionals such as your banker, investment counselor, or accountant to recommend a lawyer who specializes in estate planning.

- Contact local bar or lawyer referral services. You can locate these by calling the bar (legal) association in your community.

- As a last resort, check a directory such as the Martindale-Hubbell Directory (available in most libraries), which lists lawyers by geographical area; or check the telephone yellow pages for a list of lawyers by area of specialization.

As soon as you sit down with your lawyer, determine what the fees will be and what manner of payment will be expected. Demonstrate confidence in your attorney by freely discussing all necessary information. Time is of the essence in most legal matters; more complications can arise with each passing day. The earlier you see your lawyer and the more you cooperate, the more likely you will be to achieve satisfactory results.

A tax accountant will help to minimize your estate tax liabilities. It is wise to confer with your accountant before retirement to learn the specifics about tax breaks after retirement. If you plan to work after you become eligible for Social Security, you can consult a tax accountant to help you determine how working will affect your after-tax income and your Social Security benefits. A tax accountant can also determine the advantages of tax-deferral investment plans, such as a Keogh plan for the self-employed, an Individual Retirement Account (IRA), or a 401(k), among others.

A banker's advice can be useful in formulating your overall plan, and such advice should be sought specifically when it comes to trust arrangements. An insurance agent can help you review not only your life and health insurance needs in retirement but also your liability, homeowner's and auto insurance, all of which are necessary to help protect your assets.

Recently, a new practitioner has come on the scene: the financial planner. Many financial planners have been trained in matters relating to estate planning and can offer sound advice, though a lawyer should still provide the final guidance. Some financial planners, however, are more intent on selling financial products such as insurance policies, mutual funds, and tax-sheltered programs, for that is how many of them earn their living.

The field of financial planning is virtually unregulated, and you could be in serious jeopardy if you wind up in the hands of an unscrupulous person who calls him or herself a financial planner. So it is absolutely essential to exercise the utmost care in retaining the services of a financial planner. Check background, personal references, and professional references. Before you buy any product from a financial planner, it would be wise to get a second opinion from someone who isn't selling anything.

Anyone can call him or herself a financial planner, qualified or not, ethical or not. The following organizations represent people who offer financial planning services. You can learn more about the credentials of a so-called planner by inquiring of these associations.

American Association of Financial Professionals
P.O. Box 1928
Cocoa, FL 32923
(305) 632–8654

College for Financial Planning
9725 E. Hampden Ave.
Denver, CO 80231
(303) 755–7101

Institute of Certified Financial Planners
Two Denver Highlands
10065 E. Harvard Ave., Suite 320
Denver, CO 80231
(303) 751-7600

International Association for Financial Planning
Two Concourse Parkway, Suite 800
Atlanta, GA 30328
(404) 395-1605

Dealing with a representative from any of these associations does not guarantee that you will be satisfied. But it can be better than dealing with someone who has no such credentials.

The Cost of Professional Advice

Attorneys at law might set their fees according to the time devoted to the job, the difficulty of the job, your ability to pay, or a combination of these factors. Many lawyers charge by the hour, including both research and consultation time. In some cases a lawyer may base charges on a percentage of the amount at stake, such as in personal injury matters or real estate transactions. Court costs, filing fees, and other out-of-pocket expenses are usually added to the hourly or percentage fees a lawyer charges.

Time is the key element in legal fees. Wasting a lawyer's time is costly. It's a good idea to find out in advance what information you need to bring so that you have the relevant facts and figures in hand when you visit your lawyer.

Accountants usually charge on a per-hour basis. In some cases they may charge a set fee. Always determine the fee structure beforehand. Insurance agents usually don't charge for their counsel. A good agent should be willing to talk to you for a reasonable time knowing that you are comparison shopping. Remember, though, insurance agents earn a commission from the company with whom they place a policy.

Bankers also do not charge for counsel. Seek out and cultivate a rapport with one. Obviously, you should be a customer of the bank; all you have to do is open an account. If you contemplate a trust arrangement, confer with your banker about charges for such services.

A financial planner may charge anywhere from $500 to $5,000 or more for a master financial plan. Some financial planners will provide advice on specific topics, rather than a whole plan, for $50 to $150 or more an hour. While some planners charge a set fee for their work, others earn their living from commissions on the financial products—such as stocks, bonds, mutual funds, and insurance—that they sell their clients in connection with their planning. Planners working on commission may be less objective in their recommendations than those who do not earn such commissions.

In choosing any of your advisors, it is wise to seek recommendations from others who have used their services.

How Estates Are Taxed

The Economic Recovery Tax Act of 1981, which took effect the following year, gradually phases out estate taxes for all but a very small percentage of the population. Nevertheless, you should know that the following tax liabilities are possible.

- The IRS levies a tax (unified estate and gift tax) on certain transfers of wealth other than between spouses.

- Some states may levy an estate tax.

- Some states levy an inheritance tax, payable by the recipient of the inheritance.

- If you receive an inheritance, the amount received is *not* subject to federal income taxes. If you invest your inheritance, income from the investment is taxable, as is profit from the sale of the investment.

- If you receive property as an inheritance (such as stocks or a building), and you sell the inheritance, the gain realized can be taxable. Any earnings generated by that inheritance may constitute taxable income as well.

Taxable transfers. The unified federal estate and gift tax is levied on so-called taxable transfers: money and real or personal property that a person has passed along, either in the form of trusts and gifts while alive, or through estate distribution after death.

Gross estate. An estate is usually valued as of the time of death, but under certain circumstances, it may be valued six months after death or at close of probate. The gross estate generally consists of all that the individual owned, plus all that was owed to him or her. This can include a home, investments, proceeds of life insurance policies owned by the decedent, personal property, money due under pension and profit-sharing plans, and business interests. Jointly owned property may still be included in the gross estate under certain conditions. One-half of property owned jointly by husband and wife is usually included in the gross estate.

Taxable estate. From the gross estate are subtracted the debts of the decedent as well as expenses such as funeral and burial costs, charitable bequests, and the costs of administering the estate. When the appropriate deductions (discussed later) are subtracted, the result is the taxable estate.

There have been major revisions to the federal estate and gift tax laws in the last few years. Of particular importance are the revisions effective in 1982. It is advisable to review any wills, trusts, or other forms of estate planning that were completed before those changes were made.

Estate Planning Devices

Certain devices help you to reduce the taxable portion of your gross estate. It is important that you check current tax laws as they apply to your own estate situation.

Marital deduction. The marital deduction consists of gifts and bequests to the surviving spouse. For deaths occurring prior to 1982, there were limits on the maximum allowable marital deduction. But for deaths in 1982 and after, those limits were removed. (This change is not automatic; a will must be changed for the estate to benefit from it. Remember, though, that when the surviving spouse dies without having remarried, no marital deduction will be allowable.

Unified tax credit. After the marital deduction, a substantial portion, if not all, of a remaining taxable estate may pass tax-free as a result of the credit against taxes on gifts and estates. The credit increases yearly until 1987, when a taxable estate of as much as $600,000 will be tax-exempt.

For example, an individual dies, leaving a taxable estate of $600,000 after all allowable expenses and deductions have been subtracted from the gross estate. The tax due, before credit, would be $192,800. On deaths occurring in 1987 or later, there is a maximum credit of $192,800 allowed against the taxes. The credit thus exactly offsets the amount of the tax, so no taxes are payable on the estate. (The credit cannot exceed the tax due.)

Gifts. The unified tax credit also applies to gift giving. By making tax-exempt gifts, you can reduce the size of your estate and thereby minimize potential estate taxes. You can make gifts of up to ten thousand dollars per person per year to as many persons or organizations as you wish without having to pay federal gift taxes. If spouses join in making gifts, the annual tax-exempt limit per recipient is twenty thousand dollars.

If you make gifts in excess of the tax-exempt allowances, the excess will be considered a taxable transfer; and if it exceeds the unified credit, it will be subject to tax. Your estate will not be tax-exempt at time of death if you apply the unified tax credit to gifts given during your lifetime. However, spouses can make unlimited gifts to one another without federal gift tax consequences, although there might be state gift tax consequences.

Tax-exempt gifts and other strategies should be considered seriously by single persons, since a single person's accumulated wealth may be taxed far more heavily upon death than that of the married person whose spouse survives. It is wise for those who are single to discuss their estate tax situation with their lawyer or other advisor.

Life insurance. The role of life insurance in your overall planning changes as your children become adults and as you approach retirement age. If you have a good retirement income that will continue to support your spouse after your death, you need not carry a lot of life insurance. Rather, you should carry just enough life insurance to pay for the expenses involved in settling your estate. It is a good idea to review with professional advisors how much insurance will be needed to cover these expenses and what is the best type of policy for that purpose.

Remember, too, that life insurance policies you own will be included in your estate for estate tax purposes. Consult your advisers as to the best way to set up insurance policies to minimize or eliminate taxes and delays.

Other types of insurance—liability, homeowner's, auto—also play an important role in your estate plan. They serve to protect the various assets that make up your estate.

Property Ownership

There is no single best form of property ownership. It all depends upon your possible exposure to estate taxes and your wishes as to who should receive the property after the joint owners have died. The best solution is to discuss the matter with an attorney to determine what is right for your needs, and then to take whatever steps seem wise with regard to your overall estate plan. Consider the following four types of ownership.

Community property. Each spouse owns half the property acquired during marriage. Holdings each spouse owned separately before marriage or inherited individually after marriage are not considered community property. Eight states have community property laws: Arizona, California, Idaho, Louisiana, Nevada, New Mexico, Texas, and Washington. In states other than those, two or more persons may own property by tenancy in common, by tenancy by the entirety, or by joint tenancy with right of survivorship.

Tenancy in common. Two or more persons own shares in the property. When one dies, that share passes directly to his or her heirs, not to the other tenant. For example, if a husband and wife hold property as tenants in common, the surviving spouse does not automatically receive the deceased spouse's share. That share is subject to probate.

Tenancy by the entirety. This form of joint ownership is limited to husbands and wives and is sometimes further restricted to real estate. Neither spouse can act alone in disposing of the property.

Joint tenancy with right of survivorship. Two or more persons hold property jointly. If one person dies, that person's interest automatically passes to the other joint tenants. For example, husband, wife, and son might purchase property as joint tenants. Their reason for doing so might be to have the property pass to the surviving spouse and son, and eventually to the son alone.

Seek professional advice about the type of ownership best suited to your estate needs.

Trusts—A Valuable Tool

Trusts are among the most important tools used in building an estate plan. For the right people in the right circumstances, trusts can be an ideal way to pass wealth from one generation to another. Basically, a trust offers a plan by which a trustee (often a bank) holds your assets for your benefit or that of your beneficiaries.

You may wish to transfer thirty thousand dollars to one of your children, but you are concerned that the child might not handle the money prudently. If you want to pass that money along now, not later, you can establish a trust. If you do so with a bank as trustee, for instance, the bank/trustee will hold the money for your child in accordance with written instructions, which you may wish to have your lawyer prepare. If you want the income from the fund to be paid to your child annually, the bank will see to it. If you want the money paid out in installments or in a lump sum at any stated time (such as when the child reaches a certain age or upon your death), the bank/trustee will see to that, too. The trustee receives a fee, and you receive the satisfaction of knowing that the matter is being handled properly.

Trusts may be living or testamentary, revocable or irrevocable. A living trust is one that is set up and takes effect while the parties are living. A testamentary trust, which is created by will, takes effect upon death. For example, your life insurance proceeds could flow into a trust fund upon your death and subsequently be managed by the trustee, who may or may not be a beneficiary.

A revocable trust can be revoked or canceled by the person who established it. An irrevocable trust cannot be terminated.

Two living trusts to consider in estate planning are a *life insurance trust* and a *Clifford Trust*. A life insurance trust is set up to receive the proceeds of life insurance policies. It makes cash available to the executor so that he or she can begin settling an estate and provide income for the family of the deceased during probate. The creator of the trust can give discretionary power to the trustee, who then can make the principal available to the family to meet its needs.

A Clifford Trust is an irrevocable trust that is generally set up for a specific purpose, such as to pay for a child's education. At the end of a ten-year period, the trust's assets are returned to the creator of the trust to be included in his or her gross estate. The 1986 Tax Reform Act severely limits the tax benefits formerly available through Clifford Trusts. Check with your own tax adviser for details.

Trusts are not for everyone. An estate should be large enough to justify the payment of trust management fees. Furthermore, the initial costs of establishing certain kinds of trusts can be substantial. The offsetting benefits should be discussed in detail with your attorney and the trust officer of your bank or your financial adviser before you take action.

SPECIAL CONSIDERATIONS IN ESTATE PLANNING

The facts are simple: women generally outlive men. So the odds are strong that most married women will eventually be widows for a period of time. Sweet peace, the gift of God's love, coupled with good financial planning can make it easier to cope with widowhood.

Women in the World of Investment

"My husband took care of all our financial affairs while he was alive. But since his death, I have not known what to do!"

It is a fact of life that women outlive men and that women have not always shared in the duties of family financial management. As a result, widows are all too often left in dire straits, both psychologically and financially. They can be easy prey for swindlers and victims of well-intended but poorly informed friends who urge them to invest their money unwisely.

Start now to work with your husband toward a common end. Find out how the death of either partner would affect income flow and how it would affect expenses.

You may be widowed and alone after many years of marriage. You may be single, well into your twenties or thirties, or beyond, as you build your own career. You may be happily married but a breadwinner in your own right.

Married or single, most women today hold paying jobs. Some 55 percent of all married women were in the work force in 1985, up from 41 percent in 1971. Working wives, overall, contribute more than 28 percent of their family's total income; wives who work full-time contribute an essential 39 percent.[1]

Managing money need not be complicated. If you take it one step at a time and seek expert advice when necessary, you will be able to take charge of your own affairs. It's particularly important that you take the time to manage your money well because you, as a woman, have special needs.

- You may have to manage on less money than your male counterpart, since women in every occupational field earn less on the average than men. Some fields show greater differentials than others, but a woman, on the average, earns about sixty-eight cents for every dollar earned by a man.

"It is a fact of life that women outlive men and that women have not always shared in the duties of family financial management."

- You will probably live longer than men your age—an average of seven years longer, according to actuarial tables—and will have to provide for a longer old age. You are likely to spend those later years alone, because women outnumber men three to two in the over-sixty-five age group, and nearly two to one among those over seventy-five. In 1984, more than 51 percent of older women were widowed, compared to 14 percent of older men.

- Your pension and Social Security benefits are likely to be less than a man's, because you've probably been in and out of the work force while you took time to raise your children. Women are working more years than ever before, but the average man can still expect to work for thirty-seven years and the average woman for twenty-seven years. Many women, moreover, work in sales and service positions that often do not offer pension programs.

- If you are married and earning your own income, you will have to choose between Social Security retirement benefits based on your own earnings and Social Security retirement benefits based on your husband's earnings. You may choose the larger of the two benefits, but you may not have both.

Many wage-earning women, as a result, find that Social Security pays them no more in retirement benefits than they would have received if they had never worked outside the home.

- The Social Security benefits you receive on your husband's earnings record may be inadequate. Under current Social Security provisions, at age sixty-five, wives of retired workers are entitled to 50 percent of their husband's benefits. Widows may receive 100 percent of their husband's benefits at age sixty-five. But benefits claimed before age sixty-five are actuarially reduced.

- If you separate from your spouse and have not worked outside the home, you will be particularly in need of financial know-how. One study found that a woman's standard of living declines by 73 percent in the first year after divorce, while a man's standard of living increases by 42 percent.

Whether you are currently married or single, in your twenties or in your fifties, you need to know how to manage money in an increasingly complex world. You need a financial plan. First, however, you have to know what you want and what you already have.

The grief and confusion at the death of a spouse can cloud the common sense of a newly widowed person, which in turn can interfere with financial well-being. Sometimes widows are faced with the need to manage a fairly large sum of money, and some may not be prepared for the task. For example, statistics indicate that the average widow spends her husband's life insurance proceeds in about two years. There are several reasons for this.

- The average amount of life insurance carried is equal to only about two years' worth of income. Still, prudent management of the insurance proceeds could help stretch it out over a longer period.

- Widows may be victims of their own lack of financial experience. In some families the wife handles the day-to-day budget, but the husband assumes responsibility for the family investments.

- Widows may become victims of unscrupulous con artists who prey on their grief and confusion.

It might be a good idea for a newly widowed person to take a very conservative position in financial matters for at least a year or two, until there has been a chance to regain full composure and also do some homework on how to make the money work best. The newly widowed should choose federally insured savings plans or other safe investments rather than taking advice from those who would put their money to work at greater risk.

Having Joint Bank Accounts

While there is much to be said for a joint bank account, certain considerations should be kept in mind concerning its place in your estate. Since the money in the account legally belongs to either one of the joint owners, either one can empty the account. If a single person's relationship with his or her co-owner goes sour, or a husband or wife wants out of their marriage, either partner can take the money and run.

Even if you and your co-owner maintain a good relationship, there might be problems upon the death of one owner. With the passage of the Economic Recovery Tax Act of 1981, each spouse is assumed to own half of any joint asset. But the surviving co-holder spouse may find him or herself temporarily short of funds, since some states require that an account be frozen pending processing of estate matters when one co-holder dies. It would be wise to see what the procedure is at your bank.

For co-holders whose relationship is not that of husband and wife, the total sum in a joint account belongs to the first to die, and the total is counted in the valuation of the estate for estate tax purposes.

A Will Shows the Way

Your will is the keystone of your estate plan. This legal document—when properly prepared, witnessed, and signed—makes certain that the courts will respect your wishes. A will directs how you want to distribute your assets. If you die without a will (*intestate*), the state in which you had your principal residence at the time of your death will determine how your assets will be distributed—perhaps against your wishes.

When a person dies intestate, the court appoints an administrator to oversee and manage the affairs of the estate. The administrator's duties can include distribution of assets and naming of guardians for children or the elderly. The administrator is someone of the court's choosing, not yours. The court may require the administrator to be bonded to ensure proper performance of the duties. The price of the bond, plus the administrator's fees and other legal fees, can cost your estate dearly—as much as 5 to 10 percent of your probated assets.

On the other hand, when a person draws up a will, he or she names an executor (in some states, called a personal representative) to carry out the responsibilities of estate settlement. The executor is someone you choose, and you may elect to have him or her serve without bond. Powers granted to the executor (such as the right to sell property) can ease the processing of estate matters and minimize court appearances and costs.

The duties of an executor can be extensive, especially if the estate is complex. Choose an executor with care, making certain the person chosen is both willing and able to serve. It is sometimes wise to designate co-executors—an individual or individuals in whom you have personal trust and a bank or an attorney with the needed legal and financial expertise.

To be valid, a will must comply strictly with every requirement of the law of your state. This includes the language, the way it is signed, and the number of witnesses (two in some states, three in others).

---

*"If you die without a will, . . .
the state in which you had your
principal residence at the time of
your death will determine how
your assets will be distributed—
perhaps against your
wishes."*

Preparing your children. The shape of your estate plan can help shape your children's lives and their subsequent estate plans as well. How much do you want to provide for them, now or in the future? How much can you afford to provide without cutting into your own pleasures, comforts, and security? You should answer these questions in your own mind and then communicate your thinking to your children. Children who anticipate an inheritance that never materializes, or who did not expect one that in fact does materialize, might shape their lives differently if they had known what to expect.

A will for each spouse. If you are married, both you and your spouse need to draw up valid wills, because both of you own property: your home, car, personal possessions. One of you having a will does not eliminate potential problems. For example, a husband and wife are in a car accident. The husband dies instantly, leaving everything to his wife. She dies several days later without a will. Her estate will be distributed according to state intestacy law. If the couple has no children, the estate will probably go to the *wife's* relatives.

Hazards of do-it-yourself wills. Don't attempt a do-it-yourself will, either one you write yourself (*holographic*) or a printed form. Only about half of the states recognize such wills, many of which contain imprecise language that breeds misunderstanding. A close family member who has been disinherited may be able to successfully attack a homemade will in court and have the entire document declared invalid. The estate may thus end up being distributed according to the laws of intestacy, and the person the decedent wanted to disinherit may receive a large portion of the estate!

The cost of having a lawyer prepare a simple will need not be expensive. In terms of peace of mind alone, it may be well worth the investment.

The proving of a will. Except for jointly owned property passing to the survivor, life insurance proceeds payable to named beneficiaries, United States savings bonds with designated beneficiaries, and certain trusts, *all* the belongings of the deceased are subject to a process known as *probate*. Probate means to prove the will—to prove that the document bearing your signature is a genuine statement of how you wish your estate distributed.

In the probate process, the survivors may have to go to probate court (also called orphans or surrogate court) to present the will. Witnesses may be called in to testify to the will's execution, and the executor must satisfy the court that all bills have been paid, that state and federal death taxes (if any) have been paid, and that creditors of the estate have been notified and given an opportunity to present their claims.

Once the probate procedure has begun, the court may grant the survivors an allowance drawn from the assets of the estate. Beyond that, assets, including savings accounts and safe deposit boxes, may be frozen until the probate process is completed. This process could take a year or more. Only after all outstanding bills are paid and the executor has satisfied the court that all other costs and taxes have been settled can final distribution of the estate be made to the heirs.

You can't beat probate unless you don't leave an estate, or unless you have distributed your assets while alive. Even joint ownership does not always exclude assets from probate. Probate costs money for attorney's fees, appraiser's fees, court costs for filing papers, and bonding fees (unless the executor is authorized to serve without bond). Added to these expenses are any federal and state estate taxes, which are paid from the proceeds of the assets of the deceased; some states levy inheritance taxes, which are paid by the recipient of the inheritance.

Where should you keep your will? People have stored wills behind paintings and under rugs. Unfortunately, if the originally executed document can't be found, the court may decide that you destroyed it, intending to revoke it. You may want to have your lawyer keep the original will or even a copy. Keep copies in your safe-deposit box or with a relative. Be aware, however, that some states require that a safe-deposit box be sealed at the renter's death.

A living will. With the growth of medical technology, a document known as a living will is growing in popularity. In a living will, a person states, while competent to do so, that he or she does not want life prolonged by artificial, extraordinary, or heroic measures. This type of will must be signed and dated before two witnesses to ensure that it was signed of the individual's free will, not under pressure. The living will is a document separate from your regular will; it does not involve disposition of your property. You should give a copy of the living will to your doctor as well as to anyone likely to be involved if a situation such as that described in the will should arise.

Thirty-four states and the District of Columbia have passed legislation making living wills legally binding. It's a good idea to review your living will once a year, redating and initialing it to show that your wishes are unchanged. Some states require that this review be done within a specified number of years.

Estate Planning Checkups

Once you've made a will, don't put it away and forget about it. Review it from time to time to make sure that a revision of tax laws or a change in your status or the status of your assets or heirs won't affect the terms of your will. For instance, you may need to modify your will if you can answer yes to any of these questions:

- Have you been married, divorced, separated, or remarried? Has your spouse died?

- Have any of the beneficiaries died?

- Are there any new additions to your family or the families of your heirs?

- Has your executor died or moved away?

- Have you changed residency? (If you've moved to a new state, your will should conform to the laws of the new state. You must establish legal residence in the new state, especially if you maintain a residence in the state from which you moved. Both states could claim a share of your estate.)

- Have there been any changes in federal or state laws that might affect your will?

- Have your assets increased or diminished? If you have specified a certain sum to a beneficiary, will there be enough money to cover the bequest? (You may want to make bequests as percentages of the total.)

- Have you changed your mind about any of the beneficiaries? (In some states, if you fail to mention an heir, that heir may still be entitled to a share of your estate.)

OTHER LEGAL CONSIDERATIONS

While most considerations thus far in chapter seven have been concerned with estate planning, there are many other activities and situations that require some understanding of the law. Even if you think you know the specific law that applies to your situation, you might wish to ask a lawyer's help in interpreting and applying the law properly. Following are some common and not-so-common situations that have legal ramifications.

Making a Contract

The most common legal involvement for most people concerns contracts. A contract is made when (1) someone makes an offer and (2) someone else accepts. For a contract to be enforceable, the participants must agree to exchange something of value—money for services, for example. The details of that agreement are usually spelled out in a written, typed, or printed document.

When we sign contracts, our legal rights and obligations become firmly established. Contracts can include insurance policies (life, health, property, auto); banking arrangements (savings and checking accounts, safe deposit boxes, loans, savings certificates); charge accounts and credit cards; and agreements to buy, sell, or lease property.

Under the laws of most states, the following types of contracts must be in writing to be fully and legally binding on both parties.

- A contract extending for more than one year (such as guitar lessons for fifteen months) or one that is lifelong (such as lifetime support of someone).

- An agreement made in preparation for marriage (a prenuptial agreement).

- A loan contract with a bank or finance company.

- An agreement to establish a trust or an agreement conveying or assigning a trust in personal property.

- An agreement to employ the services of a real estate agent.

- Any contract for the assignment of a life, health, or accident policy or a promise to name someone beneficiary of such.

- A contract to sell any interest in real property or to lease it for more than a year.

Never sign a contract without filling in or crossing out the blanks. (In some states an installment contract with blank spaces is illegal.) A form *can* be changed after it has been filled out, provided that both parties agree to such a change. If a contract is altered, both parties should initial the changes made on the form.

Obtaining Consumer Credit

Learn what your rights are when you finance the purchase of expensive items such as cars, major appliances, or furniture. Usually, the seller will retain a security interest in that property if the buyer defaults in payment. In other words, the seller may be able to take back the goods if you don't meet your payment obligations.

Most states have adopted, with some variations, the Uniform Commercial Code. This code sets forth the rights of both seller and buyer. The seller retains a security interest in property purchased on time. In most cases the lender, banker, or merchant should be able to give you an adequate explanation of your obligations and rights. But if you have any unanswered questions, consult an attorney.

In addition, Congress has passed a number of laws designed to protect consumers, and some of them are designed especially to protect women. The Equal Credit Opportunities Act (ECOA) requires that a woman be given equal footing with a man (income and credit history being equal) when she is considered for credit-worthiness. Further, the law prohibits an individual's being denied credit because of race, religion, or national origin.

In addition to several provisions enabling married women to establish credit histories in their own names, the law contains two other important provisions. First, creditors cannot terminate your credit automatically because of a change in your marital status. They can, however, ask you to reapply. Second, the law says creditors cannot take away your credit cards when you turn sixty-two, as some credit card companies have done in the past.

"Never sign a contract
without filling in or crossing
out the blanks."

If for any reason you are denied credit and feel you are being discriminated against, here are some steps you can take.

- Demand a written explanation for the refusal. Under OCOA, the creditor must explain specifically why you have been turned down, in writing, within thirty days. The creditor's letter must also include a short description of the equal credit act and disclose which federal agency administers compliance with the act.

- Get third-party help. Your city, county, or state consumer protection agency is a good place to start. Or have a lawyer write a letter to the creditor.

- File a complaint with the appropriate federal regulatory agency. This could be the Federal Reserve, the Federal Deposit Insurance Corporation (FDIC) for complaints against banks, or the Federal Trade Commission (FTC) for action against stores and finance companies. If they feel you have a valid complaint, these agencies will either put pressure on the creditor or tell you that you have good cause for a lawsuit.

The Truth in Lending Law requires lenders and others who extend credit to quote all financing costs in terms of annual percentage rate (APR). This is true for almost all common financing transactions. Prior to enactment of this law, interest costs were quoted in a variety of ways, so that it was difficult to compare them. When you shop for a loan, be sure rates are being quoted in terms of APR if you want to keep borrowing costs as low as possible.

The Truth in Lending Law also offers protection to parties signing loan papers. In some cases borrowers now have the right to cancel a contract. In other words, if you sign the papers and then want to back out, you can do so if you take appropriate action within three days.

The Fair Credit Reporting Act gives you the right to examine your credit history at your local credit bureau. If you find that there is erroneous or misleading information in your file, the law sets forth the steps you can take to correct these mistakes. A glance at your credit file every two or three years is wise. Errors may sneak in, and a credit file with bad marks on it can weaken your credit record.

The Fair Credit Billing Law allows you to stop a creditor's demands for payment if you have a valid objection to your bill. Certain steps for accomplishing this are prescribed by law. Firms that bill you for credit accounts (credit card companies, department stores, and so forth) are required to provide you with copies of the law from time to time.

Remember, your rights are set forth in these laws, but it's up to you to pursue them. Also keep in mind that successful assertion of your rights often hinges on whether you act promptly.

"Remember, your rights are set forth in these laws, but it's up to you to pursue them."

Establishing a Credit History is not difficult for most people with a record of steady employment and prompt payment of debts. But what about the single individual—a widowed or divorced person who has to start from scratch to establish a credit rating? Here are some suggestions.

If you've got a steady job, ask your employer to put in a good word for you with the creditor (the Equal Credit Opportunity Act eliminates the need for anyone to co-sign your transaction). Another alternative is to open several charge accounts with local department stores and pay your bills on time. The best method for establishing credit reliability, however, is to borrow five hundred dollars or so from a bank or finance company and pay it back on time. Put your borrowed money in a savings account. This method will cost you a modest sum in interest payments, but it will provide you with a solid recommendation for future borrowing.

Setting Up a Business

If you establish a small or at-home business, you might be affected by several local laws—zoning restrictions, licensing fees, labeling and food laws—as well as federal laws, particularly federal tax laws. Your lawyer can help you interpret these laws and explain how they apply to you. If you don't find the right professional assistance at the right time, you could be throwing money away. You will need a lawyer to help you wade through leases and contracts; you will need an accountant to help you determine the financial feasibility of any given proposal; you will need the help of your banker to determine how much you can afford to invest in a given venture; and you will certainly need the services of an insurance agent to guide you through the maze of liability hazards and other businessrelated risks. Even with all that professional assistance there is no guarantee that a business venture will succeed. But without this kind of planning, success is even more elusive.

Obtaining Pension Information

Pension plans today are many and varied. Employees should be aware of the provisions of their company's plan and any changes that may occur in it. The Employee Retirement Income Security Act (ERISA) requires employers to provide their covered employees with a simple explanation of their plan. If you have questions, see your company's benefits manager.

Entering a Second Marriage

If you marry late in life or for a second time, your present heirs and your new spouse might be concerned as to how the marriage will affect their inheritance. One way of settling such matters may be to draw up a prenuptial agreement—a written contract between you and your prospective spouse signed *before*, and in contemplation of, marriage. Such an agreement can spell out precisely who owns what and can also allay the concerns of children of previous marriages.

For the best protection of all concerned, both parties to a prenuptial agreement should be represented by separate legal counsel; and a full disclosure of each party's financial status should be made to the other party. Lacking these precautions, a disgruntled party could more easily challenge and upset a prenuptial agreement at a later date.

Caring for an Ill or Incompetent Person

If you have a relative or friend who is unable to handle personal affairs because of illness, injury, mental weakness, intemperance, or drug addiction, you may petition the court to appoint you as a guardian or conservator. Different state laws set forth specific rights and duties and define how one might qualify for either a guardianship (for a child) or a conservatorship (for an adult).

Depending on the circumstances, your duties and obligations may include handling the financial affairs as well as the personal needs of the individual. Considerable responsibility may be involved. Your decision to care legally for another should not be made until all legal and personal ramifications are totally understood. Conservatorship and guardianship end when the ward regains the ability to handle his or her personal affairs, or when that person dies.

Another way to help relatives or friends is to have them sign legal documents (drafted by a lawyer) that allow you to act as an agent in certain matters. A *special power of attorney* limits you to one specific purpose; a *general power of attorney* authorizes you to transact business in general for the person.

Usually, a power of attorney terminates when the person who gave the power dies or becomes legally incompetent. In some states, though, it is possible for a durable power of attorney to be created that will continue in force (or begin to take effect) even if the giver of the power becomes incompetent.

Becoming Incapacitated Yourself

A power of attorney can be an especially valuable tool for single persons in the event of extended disability. If, for whatever reason, you are unable to act on your own behalf, someone you trust should be able to take care of matters important to you. These matters could be as simple as writing or endorsing checks or as complex as selling real estate.

A power of attorney can be given to anyone you choose, not just to a lawyer; but a lawyer should definitely draw up the documents. A power of attorney can be specific or general in scope. Since a general power is very broad, it should be given only in the most compelling circumstances.

Your welfare or that of a close friend or relative is too important to leave to guesswork. If the need for care arises, discuss with your legal and financial advisers beforehand the advisability of a power of attorney or a form of guardianship.

If You Can't Afford a Lawyer

If you can't afford a lawyer, contact your local legal aid society. Many communities have legal aid societies and clinics (check the telephone directory) that provide lawyers to persons who could not otherwise afford them. In some cases you might be asked to pay court costs. Also, federal and state governments fund legal services to provide legal help for those below an established income level.

Check local law schools. Some law schools maintain legal clinics where students (under proper supervision) serve the public.

Contact the government. City, state, and federal agencies oversee many aspects of our day-to-day affairs, such as wage and hour boards which see that fair labor practices are observed by employers. Other agencies assure and protect our rights in areas such as banking, commerce, and trade.

Make use of small claims courts, if necessary. Small claims courts in most localities can assist individuals in pursuing their rights and getting their money when amounts below an established (usually modest) dollar level are involved.

Check local human resources agencies. If you are receiving assistance from a public agency, that agency might be able to provide you with legal services. Also, numerous organizations exist to protect the rights of older persons, women, and minority groups.

Where to Write for Vital Records

To provide access to data and information relating to the health of the nation, the National Center for Health Statistics produces a number of publications containing reference and statistical materials. For information write:

> National Center for Health Statistics
> U.S. Department of Health and Human Services
> Public Health Service
> Centers for Disease Control
> National Center for Health Statistics
> Hyattsville, MD 20701

LIVING FREE

Leave the flurry
To the masses;
Take your time
And shine your glasses.

Shaker Verse

Nothing sums up retirement quite as perfectly as the word *freedom*. The biblical secret for prosperity is to live with an open, generous hand toward all, including yourself. Horace Whittell, Gillingham, England, set a good example. On the day he retired he took along to work the alarm clock which had jarred him awake for forty-seven years. He placed the clock on a concrete walkway, climbed into an eighty-ton steam roller, and roared over old faithful. He told the gathered reporters, "That was a lovely feeling."

Freedom is, indeed, a lovely feeling. It's the first thing we seek as newborn babies. My own children objected to any restraint, and well they might have. They wanted to be liberated from the playpen, then the nursery room, then the house, and finally the yard. It's all part of God's plan.

Every person who retires learns quickly what Richard Armour discovered. This writer of humor, who lived in

Claremont, California, for many years until his death in the late eighties, wrote:

> Retired is being tired twice, I've thought.
> First tired of working, then tired of not.[1]

Two ladies were discussing the freedom retired people have to do just what they want to do. One said, "You know, I am not that old, yet. I still can do just what I want to do." The second lady said, smiling broadly, "Well, my case is different. I am past the age when I can do just what I want to do!" One of my greatest joys in retirement is not only that I can do what I want to do but that I can do it in the way I want to do it. I have only two requirements: the first is to fulfill the requirements of God; the second, to fulfill the demands of my own clear conscience.

At eighty years of age, Rubenstein, the pianist, was told that he was playing better than ever. His response was notable.

> Now I take chances I never took before. You see, the stakes are not so high. I can afford it. I used to be so much more careful. No wrong notes. Not too bold ideas. . . . Now I let go and enjoy myself . . . .

Living happily in retirement depends upon continual emotional and spiritual growth. No one can remain stagnant and live free. Human beings either move ahead or go backward; they cannot stand still. That is especially true in retirement. A man who retires and does nothing just irritates his wife. Quarrels pile up. Activities together are strained. A mature wife understands what is happening and does something about it. She plans a lot of activities for herself outside the house and encourages her husband to do the same.

*"Human beings either
move ahead or go backward;
they cannot stand still. That is
especially true in retirement."*

SOME DANGEROUS FEELINGS

In order to live free, problems must be identified and solved. A lot of retired people don't have much to be happy about. Pastor Charles R. Swindoll, in a sermon to his congregation at the Evangelical Free Church of Fullerton titled "Gray Hairs, Few Teeth, Yet a Big Smile," addressed four problems which often plague senior citizens. After watching his own father die slowly and sadly, he ascertained that the following feelings invade the golden years.

"I am in the way . . . ." Feelings of uselessness often spoil life for seasoned citizens. People who were the most resourceful in their earlier years and who were looked upon for leadership and direction are hit the hardest.

In Detroit, a veteran of World War II who had retired from the assembly line grew increasingly sullen about his nonproductive life while his family were engrossed in their careers. One day he left a note on the refrigerator and disappeared. His body was found several days later in the river.

An operator of large road-grading equipment lost a leg to cancer and had to retire early. The idle hours were too much for him as he saw his fellow workers moving ahead with a growing, dynamic company while he sat, retired, on the sidelines. The misery was more than he could bear. He, too, found asphyxiation the preferred exit from his misery just ahead of a party arranged in his honor by his family and fellow workers.

"I have fouled up my life . . . ." Memories constantly peck away at the life of retired people. "I have fouled up my life," they say. "I blew it. If only I could live my life over. . . . I would pursue another profession . . . I would handle my money differently . . . I would enjoy my leisure . . . ." If only . . . if only . . . if only. . . . Hindsight is 20/20. No one can predict the future. Even those whose lives were well ordered take a turn that is later regretted.

A grandmother whose husband had died many years earlier had so mismanaged the legacy left her that she fell victim to despondency. She knew her children had counted on their inheritance, but she had fallen for a scheme set forth by a group of liars and cheats and had lost it all. Consumed by "if only . . . ," she took too much of her medicine one day deliberately and went to her reward.

"I have been given a raw deal . . . ." This feeling is accompanied by bitterness and resentment. Often it is aimed at certain people. A spouse might regret having married his bride in the prime of life. Parents might regret having children who grew up thoughtless and wandered away from the family circle. But, alas, not even God can change the past. The actions lived stand for eternity.

"I am so afraid . . . ." Many ordinary fears are intensified in the years of retirement. Older people are afraid of heights, afraid of bankruptcy, afraid of ill health, afraid of being left alone, afraid of losing their minds, afraid of dying. . . . They go to the grocery store and see the flashing red light of the UPC (Universal Price Code) mysteriously naming the item and showing its price. At the bank a computer, instead of a teller, counts out their money. Traffic lights have grown so dim it's hard to distinguish red, yellow, and green. Horns

blare on the highways when they are driving at a speed that allows them to keep the car under control.

A retired banker, sitting on a generous accumulation of savings that would have given him and his wife many rich, full years of productive life, was afraid of the years when he was no longer the man to whom his employees deferred. He,

---

> ## *"Contrary to what many people think, memory does not deteriorate with age."*

---

too, took his life. Each one of Chuck Swindoll's points above has something to do with the memory. Ah, memory. There is no more wonderful faculty of the human mind and nothing quite as certain to prod. Aristotle called it "the scribe of the soul." Without it, thought would be incoherent and chaotic. It is the most amazing vault for cherished possessions ever devised. In it each of us stores away life's relish.

Contrary to what many people think, memory does not deteriorate with age. New findings show that there are three kinds of memory, only one of which worsens in old age. Though psychologists still dispute precisely how many kinds of memory there are, most agree that there are at least three major kinds: *episodic*, for specific events; *semantic*, for knowledge and facts; and *implicit*, for skills allowing us to speak in a way that is grammatically correct, throw a ball or take a walk without falling down.

Semantic and implicit memory do not decline with age, according to Peter Graf, a psychologist at the University of British Columbia. And declines in episodic memory, he found, may be because of factors such as retirement rather than aging itself and may be reversible.

"The idea that memory inevitably deteriorates as you age came from studies that tested only one kind of memory," says David Mitchell, a psychologist at Southern Methodist University. "Now we see that there are multiple memory systems, and they each hold up differently as a person ages."

Part of the problem with the elderly, observes Daniel Goleman, writing in the *New York Times*, may be in switching attention. "If things come too quickly or in a confusing fashion, it may not register as well. But if older people are able to focus on what is happening without distractions, their memory may be just as good as ever."

FREEDOM FROM REGRETS

Memory is a fickle servant. It can bless or curse in the same hour of any day. The following three items can cause a retiree to experience tedious and tasteless hours. No one has to be their victim, however. From here on, I hope you will struggle out from under the burdens, throw them into the valley of forgetfulness, and live free.

People. Anyone who has reached the age of retirement has lived long enough to have been wronged by certain people along the way. A single unproductive relationship can mar an entire period of life. Now is a good time to commit those types to the past events and forget them.

Events. What has happened can never be altered. That includes not only the distasteful experiences but the blessings as well. Why do we always remember the bad things— earthquakes, stock market crashes, accidents, and losses? Why don't we focus instead on the wonderful reunions with friends and family, the parties, the memorable vacations?

Decisions. I know a man who spends more time wringing his hands for selling his old house too soon and losing money than he spends thanking God for his new one. Who hasn't made wrong decisions? Who hasn't gone too far, or not far enough? Who didn't step out on faith at the right time or called it faith when it was merely presumption? The enemy of our souls continues to announce our failures, our wrongs, our disappointments, and the calamities of our lives.

The prescription for these hurts is four little words. They are words from the Bible, written long ago by the Apostle Paul in his epistle to the Philippians: "Forgetting what lies behind . . . I press on . . ." (RSV). Embrace that attitude and sadness becomes joy, mourning becomes laughter.

It's what the people of Enterprise, Alabama, experienced many years ago. The boll weevil destroyed their cotton industry so they planted peanuts and turned their ailing economy right side up. The people were so happy about the pleasing turn of events that they erected a statue to the boll weevil. Southern preacher Vance Havner observed, "All things work together for good for the Christian, even our boll weevils."

Forget the past; build a monument to the future. Cook a Thanksgiving dinner and thank God for lessons learned.

HOW TO LIVE FREE

Today is the day to turn that little switch in your mind from "negative" to "positive." Take your cue from Ecclesiastes 11:8, "If a man lives many years, let him rejoice in them all." How can this be done?

Don't fear risk. To give your love to another is to take a risk; to withhold love is worse. When you give yourself to a marriage partner you are taking a risk; not to take the step is to experience loneliness. To enlist for voluntary service is to risk things not working out; not to volunteer is selfishness. Life is full of risk.

Trust others. My friend Assistant Los Angeles Police Chief Robert Vernon has carried his badge with honor for more than thirty-five years. One day in the line of duty he trusted his partner and saved a man's life.

The two officers rushed a house where a notorious gangster had been spotted. While his friend went to the back of the house, Bob rushed the front door with his gun drawn. Inside, both officers spotted at the same time the man they were after. Bob thought the man reached for his gun; his partner, from another vantage point, could see that the man with reflex action was only grabbing for a bar of soap that had slipped out of his hand. "Don't shoot, Bob!" he yelled, so Bob held his fire and saved the man's life.

Don't expect immediate rewards. When the Bible encourages believers to cast their bread upon the water it promises that they will find it after *many* days. It is possible to give yourselves to others and never see the fruit of your work.

The grandparents of Clarence Thomas, I'm sure, were in that position. Advanced in years, they nevertheless lovingly agreed to take in their grandson living in remote Pin Point, Georgia, in the home of a sharecropper so that he could attend school and get an education. They saw their sacrifice rewarded as the grandson grew to manhood, graduated from Yale Law School, was named as a federal appellate judge, and later nominated by the president of the United States to become a chief justice in the United States Supreme Court. The journey required many long years, but each sacrifice was well worth it.

Don't hesitate. Miguel de Cervantes once observed that "by the road of by and by, we arrive at the house of never."

A retired woman in Rock Island, Illinois, dabbled a bit in writing. She fancied herself a writer of fiction and prepared a story titled "The Man in the Blue Suit" which she peddled to many publishers without success. A professor at a local college offered suggestions on how to improve it, but she didn't get around to changing it. A visiting writer from the West Coast read it in a workshop and suggested still other changes. The woman went to her grave unable to find time to make the changes that might have turned an unpublishable story into a classic.

Do it now! has been a favorite expression in our family. Each member feels smug and quite efficient when, instead of waiting for time to elapse, a suggested undertaking is imme-

---

"Now is the time to reminisce. Enjoy every minute."

---

diately tackled and completed. That special knack is usually why people ask a busy person for help if they want something done quickly.

ENJOY YOUR MEMORIES

Now is the time to reminisce. Enjoy every minute. Avoid the *if only . . .* elements of your recollections, because wishing never made anything so. The only two things we can do with the past is to learn by it and enjoy its memories.

In Greek mythology, a kindly boatman named Charon was responsible for ferrying spirits of the departed across the river Styx into the future world. Once Charon reminded a woman who came to be carried over the Styx that she could drink of the waters of Leathe and forget all her past. The woman, at first happy about this new discovery, exclaimed: "Yes, I shall drink and forget all that I have suffered!"

"And you would forget all that you have enjoyed as well," the boatman reminded her.

"I shall drink and forget all of my failures!" the woman went on.

"Yes, and all of your victories," Charon added.

"I shall drink and forget all who have hated me!"

" . . . and all who have loved you."

At that the woman stopped and gave thought to the matter. Finally she entered Charon's boat without drinking the waters of forgetfulness. The price was too high.

We are all able to choose our memories. Life's review need not be a photograph, but rather a painted portrait in which selected thoughts, feelings, experiences, and episodes are recalled that will give depth of meaning to the past. It does not mean that the portrait is less true than the photograph which gives the exact surface accuracy. The painted picture may be more true for it reveals something of the inner life as well as the surface appearance.

Until I retired, I spent little time reminiscing and was a bit critical of people who lived in the past. Now I've changed my mind. There is value in reminiscing. Older people who reminisce are less depressed than those who do not. Certain experiences in life are better understood when viewed from the past. Reminiscing is not related to intelligence or lack of it. The learned person, as well as the uneducated, can make life richer with periods of reminiscing.

A photographer named Philip Halsman was engaged to photograph the actress Anna Magnani. Eager to please her, he said, "My lens is very sharp and will show all the lines in your face." Magnani replied, "Don't hide them, I suffered too much to get them."[2]

In my writing, preaching, and service as a CEO before retirement, I sought maxims which sought to put life into a single sentence: You are what you eat. Clothes make the man (or woman). Now I've settled on one that says it best: People are what they remember.

Once when Philosopher Immanuel Kant was hurt by a man named Lampe, Kant wrote on his note pad, *Remember to forget Lampe.*

Wise recollection aids me today in my relationships with other people. A person who dwells on unpleasant experiences of his life, reviewing constantly the injustices done him (real or imagined) is not very pleasant company.

---

*"People are
what they remember."*

But, ever after, the small violence done
Rankled and ruffled all his heart,
As sharp wind ruffles all day long
A little bitter pool about a stone
On the bare coast.[3]

THE ROAD
LAST TRAVELED

. . . and a time to die.

ECCLESIASTES 3:2

*I*n Sunday School one day a small boy mentioned to his teacher that his grandmother read her Bible a lot.

"Why do you think she does that?" the teacher asked.

"Well," replied the boy, "I think grandmother is cramming for the finals."

Good for her. That is precisely what the grandmother was doing. I am "cramming," too. I don't want to be a bootblack in heaven; I want to reign with Christ.

Every sane person thinks of death. "Growing old," wrote Malcolm Muggeridge in the 24 April 1978 edition of the *New York Times*, "is just a process of getting tired. Soon I shall doze off, and then fall asleep. How beautiful to stretch oneself out!"

David Rubinoff, the violin virtuoso, toured the country for many years, captivating Americans with his artistry. At ninety, Mr. Rubinoff was still performing, especially before young audiences who were simply enthralled by the music that poured from Rubinoff's violin. Each time he played, he ended by reading a poem engraved in a watch presented to him by his friend, the late Will Rogers.

> The clock of life is wound but once
> And no man has the power
> To tell just when the hands will stop,
> At late or early hour.
> Now is the only time we own
> Love, live, toil with a will.
> Do not wait until tomorrow,
> For the clock may then be still.[1]

When my friend Billy Graham turned sixty-five awhile back he was asked for his thoughts about the occasion. He answered, "The brevity of life." We all must die. There has been one death for one birth since Creation. Unless the Lord returns in our lifetime, the people of this generation will meet the Lord and stand before the Judge of all the earth.

With aging come the inevitable losses—loss of friends and relatives, loss of employment, loss of income, often loss of health, and loss (for some) of home and neighborhood. No aging person escapes some of these losses. All suffer loss to one degree or another.

In a materialistic society, people live for the present. They tend to glorify the glitzy, and judge worth on the basis of momentary glory and deny the spiritual realities that we in retirement years recognize. People grow stronger through losses. Senior citizens have a sense of reality, continuity, and purpose beyond the present.

With each passing year in retirement, senior citizens develop increasingly a desire to communicate to a younger generation. Seasoned citizens long to tell youngsters what to reject and what to accept. The older person cries to God for strength to give younger people perspective on life, to tell them of the reality of God's love and God's presence. Unfortunately, these opportunities are few.

While celebrating the wisdom of the elderly, it is impossible to ignore the pain that some aging persons face because their bodies are deteriorating. People who are suffering often

---

"Aging is not a downhill slide. . . . We all contribute to God's kingdom until death."

---

develop a preoccupation with health problems. Although they live in pain, they seek to live beyond that pain. Aging is not a downhill slide. That's destructive thinking. It implies that those who have moved beyond their prime are in a downhill slide into incompetence and obsolescence. We all contribute to God's kingdom until death.

Let's stop stressing the negative aspects of dying. Let's no longer downplay the joy of going through the door to eternity. Christians must celebrate life. Let us teach those younger how to die without fear, without being eaten up with regret.

The Lord's first recorded miracle tells us something about divine strategy for our span of life. At a wedding in Cana of Galilee, He served the best wine last. The writer adds a kind of postscript: "This, the first of his signs Jesus did at Cana in Galilee." A sign points figuratively to something else. What Christ did back then he will do here and now. When our plans go sour, Jesus steps in with his gracious provisions and sets everything right. Things go better than before.

Apply that to our span of life. First the carefree days of childhood, then the excitement of youth followed by the responsibilities of maturity, and finally the wisdom of age which leads us at last to the Father's House. And that which is coming is better than that which was. Count on it.

Our times are in his hand
Who saith, "A whole I planned,
Youth shows but half; trust God:
see all, nor be afraid!"

Robert Browning[2]

WIDOWHOOD

The loss of a marriage partner by death is a possibility for every retired person. It happens to more women than men, because the female gender has a longer life span and usually marries a partner slightly older.

To be prepared for that sudden heart attack, fatal accident or terminal illness, let's discuss them now. By planning ahead you can more serenely deal with the loss emotionally and keep from being devastated financially. Pre-arrange as many things as you possibly can. Wills need to be made. Property should be owned in a way that is advantageous to all in the event of extreme circumstances. (This varies, but joint tenancy with right of survivorship will ensure that the remaining co-owner receives the mutually owned property.) Bank accounts and safe-deposit boxes are best registered in the *Mr. or Mrs.* form. The *or* in the agreement allows the surviving spouse to have access to funds even before the will is ready.

Our marriage vows say, *'til death do us part*, but no one is prepared for that final goodbye. In a single heartbeat a wife becomes a widow, a husband a widower. Most events offer time to prepare, but not widowhood. For marriage there is an engagement period; for parenthood there are nine months of pregnancy; for moving to a new house there is an opportunity to prepare. Not so with death. The word *widower* or *widow* frightens and confuses. "No, no. Not me," we say. Victims feel dizzy, off balance, without a compass. A period of adjustment is required.

When a person is born, we rejoice, and
when they're married, we jubilate, but when
they die we try to pretend nothing happened.

Margaret Mead

A woman member of the Association of Retired Persons wrote to AARP after she was widowed to tell her first thoughts and feelings.

When I first became a widow, I hated to leave my apartment for fear that "it" showed. . . . How much I was hurting, how unjust my life was, how alone I felt. Surely, people could see all that when they looked at me. Surely, they could see that I was different.[3]

The trauma of passing from wife to widow, husband to widower, is a painful personal phenomenon. The agony seems never to end because no one is there to guide you through the adjustment. You need support from friends, permission to grieve, and patience.

Counselors like to identify the stages of grief, but there is no real order to the grieving process. Wide-ranging emotions may overlap, producing shock, numbness, and a sense of disbelief. Occasionally you might hear your lost mate in another room, see him on the street, or hear her footsteps in the hall. When you realize that your mate is not going to appear on this earth ever again, depression may follow.

Mourning never ends. The time of grief and intense sorrow can become more manageable, however. Acceptance for one person I know came when he realized it didn't demand that he didn't think about his wife any longer. He accepted the fact that a part of him will mourn for the rest of his life. At the same time, he had cherished memories to enjoy, and those would never be taken from him.

Make certain that you get involved with some of the arrangements having to do with your lover's funeral. AARP's pamphlet "Final Details," (available from Widowed

Persons Service, American Association of Retired Persons, 1909 K Street NW, Washington, DC 20049) outlines these nine legal details effective in all fifty states.

1. Make funeral or memorial service arrangements. Most traditional funerals cost more than two thousand dollars and can easily cost as much as ten thousand dollars. Make arrangements that are best for you and your family. Remember that you don't need a costly funeral to show your love and respect for your spouse. The Social Security Administration and the Veterans Administration provide burial allowances. Check with these organizations; you may qualify to receive one or both of these allowances for your spouse.

2. Find any important papers your husband or wife may have had—deeds, bank books, stock certificates, a will. *Do not throw anything out.* If you don't feel up to the search, ask someone you trust to help. Don't let your fear or personal turmoil at this time jeopardize your or your family's financial future.

3. In some states, joint bank accounts are automatically frozen. Ask your bank to release your funds to you and immediately set up a new account to handle funds received after the death.

4. Secure an ample number of certified copies of the death certificate. Also, locate your marriage certificate, your spouse's birth certificate, military discharge papers, Social Security card, tax forms, and birth certificates of any minor children. These records are needed to establish claims for Social Security, life insurance, or veteran's benefits.

5. Notify the companies that insured your spouse of his or her death. Each company, if there are more than

one, needs a statement of claim and a death certificate before the surviving spouse can be paid. There are many ways insurance money can be paid out to the widow or widower. If you do not need all of the money right away, discuss with your insurance agent all of your options for being paid and choose the best for your situation.

6. Apply to your Social Security office for benefits. Social Security benefits are not automatically paid out after a death; you must apply for them. If your spouse was a veteran, apply for veterans' benefits at the nearest Veterans Administration office. Burial at no charge may be possible in an area where a national Veterans Cemetery is located.

7. Write a formal letter to your spouse's employer, union, or any other group or professional organization with which he or she may have had an association. Many of these organizations have insurance policies of which you may be the beneficiary. You may want to ask a friend to help you write these letters.

8. Advise all creditors, including issuers of credit cards, that your spouse has died. If you have any loans, find out if they are insured. If you have mortgage insurance, your house will be paid for.

9. Consult a lawyer. Your family may be very well-meaning, but they are not legal experts. Find a lawyer you trust; perhaps a friend or neighbor who is widowed can suggest a lawyer who specializes in wills, estates, and probate. Discuss fees *before* you engage any legal help.

When you suffer an emotionally devastating event the last thing you want to deal with is money matters. But money does matter, now and for your future. Try to do the best planning you can. However, postpone any decisions that can be put off until you feel better emotionally. Many widowed persons have found that postponing major decisions for at least one year permitted them to experience all the seasons of their emotions.

Ruth Jean Loewinsohn, in her book *Survival Handbook for Widows*,[4] suggests writing on one side of a sheet of paper ten things you admired about your mate; on the other side she suggests writing ten things you disliked. Keep that sheet of paper handy. The next time you are tempted to extol the saintly qualities of your spouse, take the paper out and re-read it. Through that process, the deceased becomes a real person with real faults and real virtues, who is now dead.

A wise person once said, "No winter lasts forever; no spring skips its turn." For anyone who has lost a mate, it seems that death is only an ending. But for the survivor, it must also be a beginning.

This is not a beginning most of us ever planned to make and we are not prepared. Opening our hearts and our minds to accept this most terrible loss puts us on the path to eventual understanding. Yet it is a path that we alone can make meaningful. For it is the *process* of grieving that changes us and finally permits us to emerge from widowhood to personhood.

This transition cannot be rushed. Like the spring at the end of a cold and bitter winter, it will come.

A FEAR OF DEATH

Author Tim Stafford looks at the final third of life in terms of a week. The first day is Freedom Day, the second day is the Day of Reflection. The third day is the Widow's Day, which comes with the loss of a spouse. The fourth day is Role Reversal Day, which begins when the older person needs regular help to get along. The fifth day is Dependence Day, when a person must lean on others for basic life mainte-

nance—eating, bathing, dressing. . . . The sixth day is the
Farewell Day, a preparation for death. The seventh day is the
Sabbath, a day of worship, the day of rest. The secularist sees
death as the end; Christians see it as the beginning of a new
life. For families left behind, the seventh day is a period for
recapturing the whole image of the person who has died.[5]

---

*"It is the process of grieving
that changes us and finally
permits us to emerge from
widowhood to personhood."*

Young people often mistakenly believe that the elderly
are consumed by the fear of death. They hear us joke about
old age as being better than the alternative, and read in
literature lines like Shakespeare's in "Measure for Measure."

> The weariest and most loathed worldly life
> That age, ache, penury, and imprisonment
> Can lay on nature, is a paradise
> To what we fear of death.

Most old people would claim that they do not dwell on
the inevitable. A fear of dying is rarely expressed, but the
process of dying is quite often the topic of conversations. We
would all like to get out of life without much pain, of course,
but there is no way to guarantee such an arrangement.

The more a retired person reads the obituaries, the more
prepared he is to leave this life. My father said one day, "I
have as many friends on the other side as I do here." I think
it made the prospect of death more inviting. Older people
sometimes talk to the departed, telling them about their

activities of the day, what has happened to mutual friends, and of plans for the morrow. Such visits arise from loneliness, perhaps, but also from the persistent belief that the deceased are not dead, only removed from our sight.

Another point Tim Stafford makes is that death tends to make the elderly less fearful when there are no plans to spoil.[6] Ronald Blythe wrote in *View in Winter*, that old age can be compared with "having worked hard all day and, by the time evening comes, finding that if you can manage to work just another hour you will have done all you could. The light isn't good enough to do any more, so you have to pack up. Finish."

When facing the ultimate experience, most people do not wish to discuss their emotions. They are like soldiers in a foxhole preparing for battle. There is an intense desire for privacy. Surprisingly, painful or difficult deaths are rare. In most cases, people slip away quietly, peacefully.

In the Sweet By and By

The promise of heaven is the source of enormous blessing to senior adults. The basis is not wishful thinking but trusting in the finished work of Christ our Lord for salvation. Hope is more than wishing. For more than half a century, I have experienced the confidence of heaven, even in the days when going there seemed to be a long, long way off.

What will our eternity be like with our Heavenly Father? We know that there will be no suffering, no death, and no sorrow. We shall know each other as Jesus identified Abraham and Lazarus (Luke 17:19–23). We know each other here; surely we'll have as much sense over there!

Palm Tree Christians

"The godly shall flourish like palm trees," says Psalm 92:12 ff (TLB), "and grow tall as the cedars of Lebanon. For they are transplanted into the Lord's own garden, and are under his personal care. Even in old age they will still produce fruit and be vital and green. This honors the Lord, and exhibits his faithful care. He is my shelter. There is nothing but goodness in Him!"

Ann Pugh in Houston has taught the Bible for many years. She reminds that the palm tree is stately, upright, useful and fruitful. It is not affected by outward circumstances; it grows from the heart. The palm tree never grows too old to bear fruit.

"Surprisingly, painful or difficult deaths are rare. In most cases, people slip away quietly, peacefully."

My former pastor, Ray Ortlund and his wife, Anne, wrote in their book *The Best Half of Life* something quite appropriate for us who are retired.

> Don't huddle around with people your own age all the time. . . . Then when you die, everything you know will die, too. . . . Pour your knowledge into people twenty or thirty years younger than you. Extend your life![7]

Rev. Peter P. Tschetter was a palm tree Christian. In 1975, his testimony, *Busy in the Lord's Work at Age 89*, was published by the Pacific Garden Mission in Chicago.

> Born in 1886, I turned eighty-nine on May 19, 1975. Ever since I was saved at age 20, I felt the Lord wanted me to preach.
>
> My day starts here at 4 A.M. with personal devotions. I preach six mornings a week at 6 A.M. following a prayer service. I also teach a women's Bible class five times a

week, and a men's Bible class four or five times a week. In addition, I help new converts get started in their Christian lives.

It makes me happy? I should say! I enjoy this. To me it is a delight.

Retirees sometimes complain of boredom and loneliness. God has given us the antidote for both: "Rejoice with them that rejoice, and weep with them that weep" (Romans 12:15).

Judgment Day

Universal judgment for every person should not surprise us. It happens all the time. Everyone constantly enjoys or suffers results from decisions made. This is warning enough that one's whole life, with all of its actions and extended influence, will ultimately be judged.

A final judgment is promised when Christ returns as He promised.

> When the Son of man shall come in his glory, and all the holy angels with him, then shall he sit upon the throne of his glory: And before him shall be gathered all nations: and he shall separate them one from another, as a shepherd divideth his sheep from the goats. (Matthew 25:31–22)

The choice a person makes in life about his or her relationship to God is final, now and forever. God does not want anyone to perish, and He has opened the door for all who will come to Him. Jesus said, "I am the door: by me if any man enter in, he shall be saved" (John 10:9).

The Bible does not say much about heaven. That, surely, must be for our good. But perhaps there is more in the Scriptures than we realize.

Revelation 21 and 22 offers some information. It's a new place; tears will be wiped away; death, sorrow, crying and pain will be gone forever; the power of God and the Lamb will be present; life in heaven will be full and eternal, and no evil will curse that life.

We will have fulfilling, productive assignments to enjoy without getting tired or becoming frustrated. It might be geared to the spiritual qualities we develop in this life. We

---

"How long will heaven last?
Just as long as God reigns—
forever."

---

will see Jesus as we see each other in this life. The light we will see by will come not from a blazing star nor from candlepower, but from God's own light, which is Jesus Christ our Lord.

How long will heaven last? Just as long as God reigns—forever. If you are not prepared, this is the hour to get ready. Our sin requires our death. But Jesus Christ took our place and died so that we might live. Salvation is a gift freely given to all who take it by faith.

I'll see you at the end of the road last traveled.

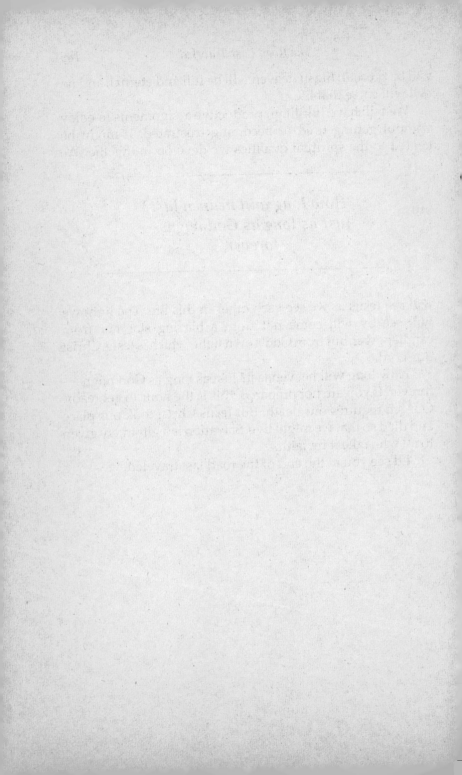

NOTES

Introduction

1. Bernice and Morton Hunt, *Prime Time*, (New York: Stein and Day, 1975), 19.
2. J. K. Hoyt, *Cyclopedia of Practical Quotations* (New York: Funk Wagnalls, 1895), 10.

Chapter 3: It's About Time

1. Ralph Waldo Emerson, *Poems of the Class of '29*, 1874.
2. Robert Lee, *Religion and Leisure in America*, Nashville, TN: Abingdon, 1964).
3. Henry Austin Dobson, *The Paradox of Time*.
4. Charles W. Shedd, *Time for All Things* (Nashville, TN: Abingdon, 1962).
5. Colleen T. Evans, "My Family Comes First," *Guideposts* (November 1965).
6. Bruce Larson, *Dare to Live Now* (Grand Rapids, MI: Zondervan, 1965).
7. Ted W. Engstrom and R. Alec Mackenzie, *Managing Your Time* (Grand Rapids, MI: Zondervan, 1988).
8. Shedd, *Time for All Things*.
9. Michael Griffiths, *Take My Life* (London: Inter-Varsity, 1970).
10. Charles Lamb, "All Fools Day," *Essays of Elia*.
11. Izaak Walton, *The Compleat Angler*.
12. J. Winston Pearce, *Ten Good Things I Know About Retirement* (Nashville, TN: Broadman, 1982), 40.
13. Sir Edward Dyer, *Rawlinson Poetry*, MS 85, 17.

Chapter 4: One for Your Money

1. *Royal Bank Letter*, vol. 72, no. 3 (Royal Bank of Canada: May/June 1991).
2. Ibid., 4.

Chapter 5: Voluntarism: The Language of Love

1. James F. Engle, "We Are the World," *Christianity Today* (24 September 1990): 32.

Chapter 6: Take Charge of Your Health

1. *Modern Maturity*, June-July 1978, published by the Association of Retired Persons.
2. Anne Avery, *Successful Aging* (New York: Ballantine, 1987), 6.

Chapter 8: Living Free

1. Richard Armour, *Going Like Sixty* (New York: McGraw-Hill, 1974), 30.
2. Pearce, *Ten Good Things*, 72.
3. Alfred, Lord Tennyson, "Guinevere," *The Poetic and Dramatic Words of Alfred, Lord Tennyson* (New York: Houghton Mifflin, 1898), lines 48–52.

Chapter 9: The Road Last Traveled

1. Pearce, *Ten Good Things*.
2. John Bartlett, *Familiar Quotations* (Boston: Little, Brown, 1980), 747.
3. James Peterson, *On Being Alone* (Los Angeles: University of Southern California Department of Gerontology).
4. Ruth Loewinsohn, *Survival Handbook for Widows (And for Relatives and Friends Who Want to Understand)* (Des Plaines, IL: AARP and Scott, Foresman, 1984).
5. Tim Stafford, *As Our Years Increase* (Grand Rapids, MI: Zondervan, 1989), 32.
6. Ibid., 228.
7. Ray and Anne Ortlund, *The Best Half of Life* (Ventura, CA: Regal, 1976).